Kingdom Buildings

Kingdom Buildings

*Your church and churchyard
as assets for mission*

Kenneth Padley

CANTERBURY
PRESS

© Kenneth Padley 2025

First published in 2025 by the Canterbury Press Norwich

Editorial office
3rd Floor, Invicta House
110 Golden Lane
London EC1Y 0TG, UK
www.canterburypress.co.uk

Canterbury Press is an imprint of Hymns Ancient & Modern Ltd
(a registered charity)

Hymns Ancient & Modern® is a registered trademark of
Hymns Ancient & Modern Ltd
13A Hellesdon Park Road, Norwich,
Norfolk NR6 5DR, UK

All rights reserved. No part of this publication may be reproduced,
stored in a retrieval system, or transmitted,
in any form or by any means, electronic, mechanical,
photocopying or otherwise, without the prior permission of
the publisher, Canterbury Press.

Unless otherwise indicated, Scripture quotations are from New Revised Standard Version Bible: Anglicized Edition, copyright © 1989, 1995 National Council of the Churches of Christ in the United States of America. Used by permission. All rights reserved worldwide.

The extract marked AV is from the Authorized Version of the Bible (The King James Bible), the rights in which are vested in the Crown, and is reproduced by permission of the Crown's Patentee, Cambridge University Press.

The Author has asserted his right under the Copyright, Designs and
Patents Act 1988 to be identified as the Author of this Work

British Library Cataloguing in Publication data

A catalogue record for this book is available from the British Library

ISBN: 978-1-78622-623-5

EU GPSR Authorised Representative
LOGOS EUROPE, 9 rue Nicolas Poussin, 17000, LA ROCHELLE, France
E-mail: Contact@logoseurope.eu

Typeset by Regent Typesetting

Contents

Acknowledgements   ix
Foreword by Bishop Andrew Rumsey   xi

Introduction   xiii

1   The theory behind the practice   1
2   Preliminaries: Planning, permission, paying, perseverance   20
3   Getting your church open   46
4   Projects that make a difference   69
5   Carbon reduction   89
6   Churchyards: From untamed jungles to sacred ground   112
7   Making the most of your church hall   135

Conclusion: Securing lasting change   157

Bibliography   161
List of images   167
Index of Names and Subjects   169

This book is dedicated to Gill, Sue, Graham, Imogen, Steph, Val, Mark, Paul and Eike: churchwardens who really got it, with whom it was a privilege to serve, and who built the kingdom in hearts and minds – assisted by bricks and mortar.

Acknowledgements

I am very grateful for those who have inspired and encouraged this book:

David Hoyle and Nick Papadopulos, who told me to write it.
Andrew Rumsey, Izaak Hudson, Andrew Rowland, Dan Crooke, Oliver Blease, John Mole, Sarah Osborne, Henry Oliver and Emily Naish, who have assisted with ideas, information and examples.
Thanks also go to John Mole for permission to use his poem on page 128.
Jackie Molnar, Charles King, Danielle Argent and Matthew Stone, who have reviewed it.
Cerys Matthews and Chris Bromley for assistance with images.
Christine Smith at Canterbury Press, who oversaw its publication.
And especially Anna and Alex Padley for their forbearance of my penchant for LED lighting and accessible toilets.

Foreword

by Bishop Andrew Rumsey

The Christian community, wrote St Peter, is a people very much like a building, where believers are 'lively stones' being formed by God into a 'spiritual house'. It's not surprising, then, that churches thereafter also became buildings that were like their people – the identification growing so close as to be problematic, with one English word sharing two meanings.

Likewise, clergy entrusted with the care of God's people usually also find themselves inadvertent curators of one or more complex, often ancient structures, in which human experience seems to have soaked into the very brickwork. They find that to move or alter anything in these sensitive places is to provoke surprisingly strong reactions, when all they were hoping to do was offer a slightly warmer environment or better grade of coffee.

Very few of those with responsibility for Anglican church buildings have been trained in or even much advised on the management of this centuries-old interplay, with the result that built heritage and Christian mission can be viewed as separate and unrelated categories, to the detriment of both. It is splendid, therefore, to welcome a book that so fluently weaves sound theology with helpful, practical know-how, and sets Christ and his kingdom as the cornerstone of our thinking about these extraordinary assets.

Kenneth Padley is to be warmly commended on writing a book that fills a long-vacant niche. He leads the reader confidently across the threshold (sometimes, the minefield) of church buildings projects, and enables, too, the wise stewardship of their neighbouring churchyards and halls.

We have needed a guide such as this; one to whom I am glad to open the door.

The Rt Revd Dr Andrew Rumsey
Bishop of Ramsbury

Introduction

This is a book about the kingdom of God. This 'kingdom' is not a place but a reality. It is the term Jesus used to describe the reign of God in people's lives. It was the unifying theme of his preaching – the first thing he announced when he began his public ministry (Mark 1.14–15), and the concept that captured his vision of men and women, young and old, in harmony with one another and their Creator. The kingdom was the idea that he enacted in his miracles as he embraced those excluded from community through illness or ritual impurity.

As this is a book about God's kingdom, we will begin with theology. Chapter 1 explores the meaning of the word 'church'. Christians use the term both for God's people and holy buildings. The two concepts are intimately connected: we will see how the mission of God's people is facilitated, enhanced and blessed when we have buildings that are fit for purpose. Appropriate hardware enables us to do the human stuff better.

So this is also a book about kingdom buildings. We will be considering places of worship as well as ancillary church facilities, such as halls and burial grounds. These resources were gifted and developed by previous generations to the glory of God, and intended to help local Christians become effective in mission by providing space for worship, learning, social action and friendship. Over the centuries, they have proved invaluable assets for their congregations and wider communities.

Too often, however, churches and halls have not been adequately maintained, and their fabric and contents have not kept pace with the changing expectations and requirements of contemporary society. Worse still, tired and crumbling buildings transmit a pervasive message that God is antiquated or irrelevant – maybe even dead. Church buildings are often cold and poorly lit. Too often, they are shut throughout the week. Many are hard to access for those with limited mobility, sight and hearing. And in an age of climate change and environmental anxiety, congregations need to be rapidly reducing their carbon consumption if they are to embody the Christian calling to safeguard the integrity of creation.

Many of these issues have been known for a long time. However, extra challenges have emerged in the aftermath of the coronavirus restrictions. The forced closure of places of worship in 2020 represented an unprecedented change for worshipping communities. For many churches, the existential threat of the coronavirus restrictions continue to cast a long shadow: it is very easy to decimate a congregation; much harder to rebuild it. Congregational decline, perceived or actual, can form a negative feedback cycle within the mentality of local communities that catalyses volunteer burnout and reduces regular giving. Acutely strained congregations are now struggling to recruit officers to vital roles and unable to meet the costs of ministry.

Within the Church of England, these changes have elicited a two-pronged response. Drawing on the biblical concept of jubilee, 'fallow time' will be proposed for churches that are fragile but not necessarily terminal. Rather than face the cliff edge of formal closure, parish status and governance would be paused and the community given a chance to rest and recuperate.

During such a period of suspension, churches will, inevitably, need financial support. So, the second prong of the Church of England's response is to scope out the possibility of forming new heritage trusts to attract a mixture of diocesan and government funding to support fallow churches. I crudely liken these heritage trusts to the 'bad banks' that were created in the wake of the financial crisis in the 2000s, the purpose of which was to rescue and restructure institutions that were otherwise unviable and potentially contagious to the whole system. Of course, the principles behind these proposed changes to the Mission and Pastoral Measure are fundamentally positive: the hope is to return churches from fallow time to operational use as bases for Christian mission and ministry.

The situation of other churches is more positive. They are bouncing back from the setbacks of the past few years with hope and vigour. Even these, however, cannot stand still. Any church that just treads water is not maintaining the status quo but is effectively moving backwards. This is because contemporary expectations are continually rising, including demands on the buildings where people worship, and which they visit and hire for parties and meetings. A church that is inattentive to shifting cultural sands will wither and die. A church that embraces these changes will acquire new people along the way. As a vicar, I saw how building projects could inspire whole communities to offer skills and energy, including those less familiar to faith, and whose involvement with fabric projects drew them deeper into the worshipping life of the Church.

Ultimately then, this is a book about building the kingdom through the buildings of the kingdom. It proceeds from the premise that, whatever the condition of your church, hall or churchyard – good, bad or ugly – there is usually something that can make a marginal improvement and take things in the right direction.

Sometimes changes are substantial and require significant periods of prayerful preparation, detailed planning and fastidious fundraising. Chapter 2 considers some of the common threads that run through big building projects: the requirement for robust plans; the hurdle of official permissions; the means of paying for them; and the need for perseverance on a sometimes long and winding road.

Moving into the heart of the book, I will be sharing examples of projects that have shaped my thinking about the effective management of church buildings. My examples are intentionally small as well as large, simple as well as complex, each distinct to context and drawn from across the topography of modern Britain: affluent as well as less well-heeled communities in urban, suburban and rural contexts.

Chapter 3 outlines the blessings of opening church buildings to visitors during the week. Chapter 4 considers projects to enhance church interiors, such as decent toilets, or which build new connections through the introduction of cafés or office space. Chapter 5 is about the crucial contemporary challenge of cutting carbon consumption. Chapter 6 asks how we can turn churchyards from overgrown wildernesses into oases of peace and welcome. Chapter 7 explores how churches can make the most of their halls for congregational events and outreach, plus community hire and a source of income for mission.

As an Anglican priest, I understand best the people with whom, and the systems and buildings with which, I work daily. I hope that what I write will speak to the situation of vicars, churchwardens, treasurers and other worshippers who help to maintain and finance their parish churches, or who hold equivalent posts in other denominations. It will be of little technical use to those who support churches as professional advisers – such as architects, archaeologists and specialist craftspeople – but it might offer a priestly perspective on the building challenges that we share together. In a related vein, while this is a book about advancing Christian mission through bricks and mortar, some of its underlying principles may also resonate with those who manage places of worship for other faith traditions, or who are responsible for secular places of gathering, such as community halls and green spaces.

This book is an exploration of how churches can build the kingdom through the buildings of the kingdom. It is written in the hope that it can sit alongside existing resources on Christian faith and life; it is a practical outworking of ecclesiology, insisting that good management of buildings is a concrete expression of the Church as community.

A flurry of recent publications and courses have been aimed at reversing declining attendance at worship and fostering growth in the local church. These resources often emphasize the importance of welcome. The imperative for a good welcome is integral to many of the projects considered in this volume, and the ways in which it can help Christian communities to grow.

In parallel, many manuals about priesthood have been written to share the joys and strains of ordained life, but few if any prepare clergy for the tasks of buildings management in which they will inevitably become embroiled. Similarly, while there is a suite of resources to support churchwardens, parish administrators, treasurers, and so on, this book offers details and examples about building projects that such aids do not provide.

I hope to build on the work of writers who have probed the intersection between theology and place, and the relationship between architecture and liturgy. At a more practical level, Nigel Walter is foremost among those who have shared their perspective as professionals charged with designing and implementing churches' building projects (Walter and Mottram; Walter, 2014; Cooper and Brown). I hope to align with these resources by bringing the perspective of a priest, integrating theological ideas and missiological principles into a study of how churches can effectively manage and modify their buildings. This book also brings the perspective of a client keen to commission projects that get the maximum return on investment at the front line of Church ministry.

The limited scope of these pages reflects the horizons of my experience and the uniqueness of every church setting. This book will not have answers for all your challenges. Each congregation and its leaders need to work out what is right in their own context. But if my examples might supply fresh perspective or energy for your situation, I will rejoice. Through an idiosyncratic mix of principles, examples and anecdotes, we will tackle topics that are true of any community building. We will also ask how the physical hardware of local churches can best equip God's people in the service of the gospel.

1

The theory behind the practice

The central premise of this book is that the care and development of church buildings can make a massive contribution to Christian mission. As we unpack this claim, we will find a combination of theory and practice, ideas and implementation. We are going to start with theory because that is the trajectory of classical Christian theology, moving from the Creator to his creatures. God leads: we follow.

The branch of theology that we need to explore is ecclesiology. Ecclesiology enquires into the nature of the Church and why it exists. After this, we can attend to missiology: a consideration of what the Church does. This in turn will help us to see where church buildings and their grounds have a role to play in Christian outreach. And once we discern this, it will become clearer that even small steps in fabric maintenance can make a positive impact on mission.

1 Ecclesiology

Church as people and building

Christian thinking about the Church starts with the notion that Church is people. This is a theological principle grounded in historical reality. Christianity was illegal for much of its first three centuries. It was an underground faith, subject to intermittent bouts of local and imperial persecution. Christians were not allowed to gather in public for worship. As a result, Christian self-perceptions of their identity coalesced around concepts of human community. The earliest articulation of this situation can be seen within the New Testament itself, although inevitably it continued long beyond the age of the New Testament. Christians lived in a state of vulnerability, impelled by a belief 'that they were strangers and pilgrims on the earth' (Heb. 11.13, AV). They sensed that the difficulties of the present age were passing and so they looked forward to the more permanent security of God's future. In doing this, despite having no public buildings, they drew on metaphors of construction. They compared their community to cities, houses and temples. Christians may not have enjoyed buildings in which they could gather openly, but they longed for a world in which that might become an outward expression of their inward identity (2 Cor. 6.16; Heb. 11.8–10; Rev. 21–22).

Unable to gather in public, Christians met in individuals' homes for prayer and praise, teaching and fellowship. A few examples of early Christian meeting houses have survived into the modern era. The most famous of these was at Dura Europos in Syria, a site tragically desecrated by ISIS in the early twenty-first century. The house church of Dura Europos was an ostensibly domestic setting, but rooms were laid out for Christian worship and teaching. Separate spaces for celebrating the Eucharist and baptism were clearly identifiable: the first indications of the furniture and functions that would characterize church buildings of subsequent centuries.

A glimpse at the earliest Christian buildings: the house church of Dura Europos, Syria.

However, no public Christian buildings were possible within the Roman Empire until AD 312. This was the year in which Emperor Constantine converted to the faith and reversed the prohibitions of his predecessors. The resulting transformation of Christian fortunes catapulted the faith into a new era of visibility and confidence. As soon as Christians were permitted to build places of worship, they set to the task. In many parts of the Empire, Christians were already strong in number. In some places, they were the largest faith tradition, or maybe even a majority in the population.

An illustrative instance of such early church architecture has recently been unearthed in Laodicea in western Turkey. The fourth-century church of Laodicea was built to accommodate several hundred people; it was laid out with three aisles, facing east, terminating in an apse, plus an entrance hall (narthex) across the back. It is a design that anticipates the layout of many later Eastern Orthodox churches. The church of Laodicea was deliberately prominent. It was placed next to the most magnificent pagan temple in the city, with the clear intention of dwarfing it. The new church was a statement of permanence and intent: Christian buildings were to rival and eventually displace the shrines of the old gods.

The advent of buildings like the church of Laodicea also laid the foundations for a transformation in the meaning of the word 'church'. For Christians, the Church was no longer just a gathering and an institution; it was also a building. This understanding of church as building has come to overshadow the earlier concept of church as people. Were we to go onto any high street of twenty-first century Britain and ask what people understood by the word 'church', they would likely identify buildings in which Christians meet together. They might point to a nearby example, perhaps a distinctive gothic or classical edifice up the road, which they recognize as a 'church'.

There is nothing wrong with such evolving etymology: language has always been pliable. Words change to suit the needs of the people who use them. The lesson that Christians should draw from this evolution is that church buildings are the shop window for church people. In the popular understanding, churches are statements in stone, wood, metal and glass: the first things that most associate with Christianity – a threshold towards beliefs and practices. Crucially, this means that the ways in which Christians present, maintain and open their places of worship will speak volumes about their views and values. A church that is scruffy, cold and inaccessible will convey a wholly different message about the love of God from a church that is warm, well-lit and uncluttered. Getting our buildings right should therefore be of high importance for any Christian community: it will reveal more than words about the gathering into which others might be invited to join.

Church as global and local

There are in fact two different words that Christians have used down the centuries to designate their corporate identity. These words have different origins and so mean different things. It is not that one is right and the other is wrong. On the contrary, both shed fresh light on each other and deepen our understanding of Christian community.

Up until now, we have been using the word 'church'. This is an Anglo-Saxon term, related to the Scottish 'kirk', which came into English from the German *kirche*. *Kirche* in turn stems from a Greek word that is used in the New Testament, *kuriakos*. *Kuriakos* means 'of the Lord'. Christians belong 'to the Lord' and so the Church is made up of those who are summoned and saved by Jesus. They meet in the name 'of the Lord' and celebrate his presence. They look to the example of the Lord and await his return in glory.

This etymology about being centred on the Lord means that 'church' is a rather top-down word. It reminds Christians that they are part of a global faith tradition, with brothers and sisters in every country on earth. Importantly, this also includes Christians in different denominations – even in different centuries, past and future, as well as here and now. As members 'of the Lord', Christians are one with those who have gone before in faith and with all who will follow: each and every Christian a saint.

I am often quizzed about that line in the creed that says: 'I believe in the holy *catholic* Church.' 'Why do you say "catholic"?' I am asked. 'Isn't the Church of England supposed to be Protestant?' 'Well, yes,' I reply. 'It is. But,' I continue, 'it is also catholic. To say that the Church is "catholic" is to affirm its universality.' The creeds and their use of the word 'Catholic' date from the early Church, long before the divisions of the Protestant Reformation. To say the Church is 'catholic' is to affirm that the people 'of the Lord' – *kuriakos* – are one. Someone who likes baroque, jazz and heavy metal might be said to have a 'catholic' taste in music. Just so, Christians are catholic because they belong to something bigger than themselves, bigger than their local congregation, bigger than their denominations, bigger even than the Church on earth.

Ultimately, the Church as *kuriakos* reminds us that God comes first and people second. God alone is eternal, the Creator of all that is. It is thus an essential role of the Church as *kuriakos* to point to the radical difference and otherness of God. Likewise, church buildings, albeit imperfect works of flawed human beings, must nonetheless witness to the greatness, majesty, perfection and sheer difference of the One who makes and saves the world. This is an awesome calling, but one in which the best church buildings, large and small, old and new, have been striving and succeeding for centuries. It is the vocation of church buildings to speak of eternity and to act as gateways to heaven. In what ways might your church be a witness to this? Are there ways in which it could do it even better?

In addition to the word 'church' from *kuriakos*, there is a second term that Christians use for their common identity. A church building in France is known as an *eglise* and in Wales as an *eglwys*. These words share a common root from which the English get 'ecclesiastical'. The origins of this linguistic family also track back to the Greek of the New Testament. Where modern English Bibles read 'church' (e.g. Acts; Paul; Rev. 1–3), the underlying Greek word is not *kuriakos* but *ekklêsia*. *Ekklêsia* is a compound term, made up of two smaller words. Together they mean 'called-from'. *Ek-klêsia*, literally 'from-called'.

Ekklêsia is a word that the first Christians adapted from secular usage. An ancient Greek *ekklêsia* was a political gathering, a folk moot. If the village over the hill was going to attack your village, you might meet with your neighbours in an *ekklêsia* to discuss a response. At such an *ekklêsia*, the people were 'called from' their daily tasks to discuss matters of common interest. So *ekklêsia* is very much a grassroots, bottom-up word: it is about people coming together at a local level – a contrast to the top-down connotations of *kuriakos*. It is not hard to see why the first Christians saw themselves as *ekklêsia*: the word describes gathering for worship, while also conveying wider inferences about salvation because Christians are 'called from' past sinfulness to lives of holiness after the example of Jesus.

Ekklêsia is therefore not only a bottom-up word but also an inherently prospective word. It looks to the future. In the popular imagination, Christianity may appear to be desperately traditional, stuck in the past, out of touch. Sadly, there are some Christians who collude with this pastiche. But the calling of Christians to be *ekklêsia* points in the opposite direction: Christians are inspired by past story but are ultimately called into God's future. As *ekklêsia*, Christians are always looking forward, always open to God's change, always affirming that the best is yet to come. A church community that is open to God's amazing future will be one that makes positive, adaptive use of its resources, including its buildings.

We have identified a complementarity between the two words that Christians use for their corporate identity and places of worship. A community that embodies the meaning of the word *kuriakos* will look to the Lord; it will value its place of meeting (whether ancient or modern) as an attempt to articulate the things of eternity. At the same time, a church that expresses the word *ekklêsia* will not rest on its laurels. It will seek to make its built heritage as relevant as possible for grassroots mission in the present day.

2 Missiology

What we have discovered about the nature of the Church is starting to have implications for Christian mission. A theory of mission – missiology – will therefore inform how Christians use, maintain and develop their buildings.

The eternity business

A church that is 'of the Lord', seeking to witness to the life of God and the things of heaven, should plan and act for the long term. Down the many Christian centuries, the followers of Jesus have placed great confidence in God's mastery of time. We see this in the willingness of Christian martyrs to pay the ultimate price in witness to the greater horizons of God's providence. And we see this in the confidence with which Christians have invested in their buildings. Whether small or large, churches have been built to last, often using the most permanent materials available and lavished with the greatest of artistic creativity. As an earthly witness to the things of heaven, Christian investment in churches points to the God of providence, whose enormity and kingdom we affirm in our creeds.

Despite this auspicious backdrop, churches today are often desperately short-termist in their care for the built environment. We know from popular anecdote that 'a stitch in time saves nine'. However, again and again, I see churches fail to prioritize repairs and upgrades, so small niggles grow into big problems that become more costly to address. Occasionally, big costly problems simply become too big and costly to resolve.

- Maybe you know the church that cut back on grounds maintenance because of a drop-off in those willing and able to maintain the gardens. It struggled to put in place alternative care for the churchyard, so bushes grew and paths deteriorated. The congregation felt unsafe walking to church: attendance dwindled and connections with the local community withered. Unsurprisingly, that church in North Wales is now closed.
- Maybe you know the church that cut itself off at the knees by selling its car park, without any plan to reinvest the proceeds in projects or facilities that might increase the congregation. The income from the sale was frittered away as a temporary cash cow. Unsurprisingly, that church in South Wales is now also closed.
- Maybe you know the church that suffered from mouldy damp on the walls of the Lady Chapel. On repeated occasions a hardy volunteer got up a ladder and painted over the damage. But the damp kept recurring. It was only when an insightful churchwarden spoke with the church's architect that the cause of the problem was identified. Lead flashing on the roof had failed with the result that rainwater was pouring through to the plaster. By taking time to investigate things properly, the source of the damage was stopped and a line drawn under the issue. The volunteer who once spent hours up the ladder with a pot of paint can now use their time more productively in the mission of that congregation. Unsurprisingly, this church just northwest of London continues to flourish.

These examples illustrate that, despite the claims of the Church to be in the eternity business, too often thinking and behaviour on the ground exposes a different reality. The long-term interests of church buildings (and to a wider extent the strategic aims of a congregation) can fall victim to more pressing concerns. There are many reasons for this. Some churches become too busy, often consumed by laudable projects, and so take their eye off the buildings in which they are ministering. In such an instance, it is the role of the leadership team to remind that church about long-term obligations alongside immediate needs.

No longer in the eternity business: a derelict chapel.

Other churches lose sight of the future because of fears about decline. Congregations can become trapped in cycles of negativity: 'change and decay in all around I see' ('Abide with me'). Churches with this mentality are more likely to accept temporary patches to their buildings, just to keep 'the show on the road'. There are instances when the costs of a proper repair are prohibitive; but a short-term approach to fabric maintenance only kicks the can down the road, postponing the day when more serious and costly interventions will be necessary.

If a church is confident on good grounds in the future of its faith community, it is imperative that it maintains and develops its buildings. If a church is genuinely doubtful about its long-term viability, might it not be prudent for the congregation to remain in control of events by seeking a period of fallow time (see p. xiv), or to close their church and pool resources with another community? The unpalatable alternative is to allow problems to stack up until catastrophic failure condemns the electrics or blows the roof off. At this point, permanent closure of the building becomes almost inevitable, leaving the faithful few who remain with limited resources and energy to merge with another community.

If Christians are in the eternity business, then churches that stand still will move backwards. By this I mean that the expectations of contemporary society are constantly changing. People of the twenty-first century demand certain facilities as standard that past generations would have dismissed as luxuries. For example, I knew a church that was facing a big, unbudgeted six-figure bill for replacing the heating system – but one worshipper queried whether the heating should be replaced at all. Their argument was that the church had not been heated when it was built in the tenth century, so maybe the congregation could live without heating in the twenty-first. Here was an argument for inertia: struggle through cold, damp winters on the grounds that this would capture the original spirit of the place. It might even be possible to dress up such caution as low-carbon sustainability. Arresting though the idea is, it is inherently flawed: only the hardiest of contemporary worshippers will turn out during the winter months to worship in a church without heating. However, I was so blindsided when I first heard of this issue that it was only days later I realized what I should have said in response. The Anglo-Saxons who first built that church were familiar with buildings that had no heating. At best they would have had a few draughty open fires in their domestic hovels. However, when I last checked, there were not many Anglo-Saxons left to evangelize. Times have changed; standards are different. If we want to do effective evangelism in the early twenty-first century, then we will need decent heating and not expect too many Anglo-Saxons to be tutting at our extravagance.

Another example came a few years later. Increasingly, our halls administrator found potential hirers enquiring about whether we could offer wifi in our facilities. There were several reasons for this: those organizing children's birthday parties wanted to use the Internet to download music; and those who were leading meetings needed to access webpages and presentations on the cloud. Had we failed to respond to these requests, we would have lost business and been left with less income to pursue the charitable objectives of the parish. Solving the lack of the Internet was not easy: none of the buildings had broadband and there were various reasons why British Telecom didn't want to link us up. In the end, we leased a 4G hot-spot box: it incurred a monthly fee, but we recouped this cost from the bookings that we retained and the new ones that we added. Being portable, the box could be deployed across any of our parish buildings as and when it was needed.

These examples illustrate how churches that are serious about being *ekklêsia* and called into God's future need to remain on the front foot as regards evolving societal expectations – in addition to their routine maintenance. Attention to these details shout loud and clear that churches are in the eternity business.

People before finance

Buildings that are fit for purpose speak about the value that Christians place on the people who might come through our doors, not just to join in worship but also to use facilities, such as our halls. And Christ has no hands on earth but ours: ultimately, the way in which we care for our buildings should speak about the value that God places upon people. Too often churches forget this if confronted by financial pressures and sub-prime fabric. On several occasions, I have seen a perverse line of argument develop that says something such as 'the Parish Share has gone up again and we need to replace the sound system: we must draw in new people so we can pay these bills'. No, you don't. A church that makes income the motivating factor for evangelism will fall at the first hurdle. New people who join churches bring with them many gifts from God: energy, ideas, money and talents. These can be utilized in due course. But that is not why we want to meet them. We want to meet new people because God loves them and Christians are charged with demonstrating this in how we relate to them.

The priority of people over finance should also inform our building projects. We live in a world of infinite possibilities. But we cannot do everything. We need to prioritize. If people come first, churches should focus on those projects that will have the biggest impact on our ability to reach a larger and wider audience over the long term. A church that budgets successfully and prays carefully about its mission should get this right. However, before a church can determine where it is headed, it first needs to know its starting point. Obtaining such a baseline assessment can be easier said than done. This is because undertaking a realistic review of where things are includes making an honest assessment of weaknesses and challenges. And there are several arguments that can distract from this important task.

- Some are tempted to delay a response, burying their metaphorical heads in the sand, trying to pretend that problems do not exist and that they will go away. This subterfuge may succeed for a short period, but it will only postpone the day when serious decisions must be made and action taken.
- Another response is to look for a scapegoat by playing the blame game. Such sleights are rarely well received and so the safest version of this argument is to cast aspersions at those who have gone before us. It is relatively easy to blame our predecessors. However, it is ungracious to malign in public anyone who has little right of reply. Moreover, blaming the past must not become an excuse for inaction in the present. Our task is to make the best use of the time and resources that we are given.
- A third way in which we may try to evade the need to start where we are is exhibited in 'blue-sky' thinking. We all know people who are animated by exciting visions of the future – but have little sense of how to get there. Most people can generate ideas about how they would like things to be; how things could be done differently. But the viability of such visions cannot be assessed until we have a full and realistic grasp of the present-day situation on the ground.

So we can only start where we are. By this I mean we need a full and honest assessment of the issues that confront us and the resources at our disposal. This is not just a matter of awareness about physical, financial and human assets; it is also about getting a deeper-seated purchase on the ethos of a place, and of discerning God's purposes for the faith community within it. There are many ways in which a church leader or leadership team can enhance their understanding of their context.

Starting where we are: people

First and foremost, context is about people. How well do you know your congregation? Do you have a sense of their passions and fears, skills and interests? Smaller churches may feel vulnerable in this regard, with few people at their disposal. However, there may be strength in such littleness: worshippers in smaller churches usually know one another well; there will be a robust appreciation of individuals' skills and gifts, dislikes and limitations. Yet even within a small congregation, there may be quieter members who hide their lights under a bushel. Such people might have considerable gifts to offer, given the right encouragement and support. Likewise, there may be those who have been tasked with one aspect of church life but whose sense of call and service could be re-energized by the challenge of swapping into a different role more suited to their skill set.

Beyond the core of any congregation, there are often those with more tangential connections to the life of a church. This group is often a fruitful one to tap and encourage. Their skills and willingness to get involved may have been overlooked because they are on the margins. Most people are honoured to be asked even if they feel they have to say no. Moreover, involving such people in a project is likely to draw them further into the life of the worshipping community.

In the case of larger congregations, there are inevitably more people to call upon. However, it is also harder to match skills against opportunities. This challenge becomes particularly acute when a congregation is too large for a single person (usually the vicar or other lead minister) to know everyone personally. This size will vary with context but, for the sake of neatness, we might set it at 100 people. I was certainly conscious of the change of scale in this regard when I moved from parish ministry to life at a cathedral. The parish in which I worked in Hertfordshire had an electoral roll of nearly 200 and a regular Sunday congregation of just over 100. This meant that I could be pretty sure when someone new was attending a service; I made a point of saying hullo afterwards and getting to know them if they had recently moved to the area or were interested in finding out more about the parish. Things are wholly different where I now work, in a cathedral: patterns of connection are more complex; attendance by some is ephemeral; and there are tens of thousands of visitors who pass through the building every month.

Even though we are blessed with a team of dedicated clergy and lay colleagues who are gifted in networking and pastoral care, we find it harder to recreate the depths of relationship that can be found in many parish churches.

This said, there are ways in which leadership teams of larger churches can keep abreast of congregational skills and interests. At the simplest level, they can pool their shared wisdom at leadership meetings. This is likely to be enhanced when a church runs a small-group (cell) network allowing regular worshippers to become well known by others in their home group. Regular meetings of home-group leaders can share some of this knowledge; then targeted approaches can be made to match skills with needs. By contrast, requests for 'volunteers' in the Sunday notices are rarely successful and run the risk of evincing an unfortunate mismatch between need and availability. Particular attention might be placed on new joiners, for example through a team of carefully selected and trained lay welcomers; or, more simply, through a line on the welcome data collection form that says, 'Do you have skills and interests you would like us to know about?' Wording such as this invites the person to reveal their aptitudes, without committing the church to taking them up on their offer. In addition, intermittent approaches may be made to the whole congregation through a 'time and talents' survey, perhaps alongside a regular giving campaign. Time and talents surveys can be onerous but, if conducted thoroughly, may pay back through the way in which they can raise the leadership team's awareness of skills within a congregation.

Knowing the people of a place is not just about an appreciation of talents and interests. It is also about insight into the self-understanding of a congregation, as individuals and communities. What stories do they tell about themselves, including about their faith and the life of their church? Are these stories accurate – or are they myths, oft-repeated, for the sake of simplicity or in a vain attempt at self-deception? What memories or legacies of history are held within a place and its community?

Andrew Rumsey's seminal study of the English parish scrutinizes the complex interrelationships that shape local communities. The ethos of any place is shrouded and formed by the intangible heritage of remembrances and perceptions. 'The place practised is a function of the place conceived' (Rumsey, p. 76). Each present-day community has powerful emotional cultures (positive and negative) that can pervade –

haunt even – its buildings and objects. Given this, there can be no quick bypass for the laborious process of deepening our awareness of the self-understanding that has cultivated the character of a place. What myths do people perpetuate about the area in which you live or the church to which you belong?

Starting where we are: social and spiritual topography

Alongside understanding the individual people of a church and their collective identities and behaviours, a church leadership team also needs a good awareness of the local area in which the church is set. This is especially true for those churches that operate a more territorial/parochial model of mission and ministry. After all, it is with the people who live and work around the church building that the church community is likely to interact most regularly. Obtaining accurate knowledge about these people is an essential preliminary to any missional strategy that a church might seek to develop. Many books and resources have been written on this subject of Mission Action Planning (see the Bibliography, pp. 163–6), so I will only skim over the headline issues as far as they affect care for church buildings.

The Internet is a good place to start a desk-top study of a local area. Data from the most recent census can provide the age profile of a given community as well as its social make-up, including indicators of deprivation. This data may be studied across regions, cities and towns. But it is also available at a parish level through an Internet search for the ARCGIS map of the Church of England. This invaluable resource provides information about each parish in the land. A close study of this information may assist a church in a SWOT analysis (strengths, weaknesses, opportunities and threats) of the local area and allow it to start to identify the directions in which it might usefully channel its energies. The ARCGIS map can also provide some comparators with adjacent and nearby communities. For example, how much should we focus on rural poverty if the ARCGIS map shows that this is an even bigger issue in the parish next door? Or might combined concern about this issue provide the fruitful basis for a cross-parish project?

Beyond the Internet, however, there is no substitute for asking real people about their perception of where the church fits into the social ecology of a place. At St Michael's, St Albans, when preparing a new strategy, our Mission Action Plan (MAP), we developed a few simple surveys to gather qualitative data from local businesses, from those involved in the life of local schools, and from those who connected with the parish through use of our halls.

It goes without saying that any exercise by a church to get a better understanding of its people and area must be undertaken within the context of prayer. It is essential for a church to commit any process of reflection on mission to God's greater purposes; this way, a church can discern the right next steps and not get blown off course by the myths that a community perpetuates, or by the demands and ideas of those who shout the loudest. Different churches will have various ways of praying about this. It might be an act of worship at the start of a parochial church council (PCC) away day to plan your new MAP. It might be a team of parishioners who are committed to interceding regularly for the leadership team as it develops the new strategy. Whatever is right for your context, grounding the exercise in prayer is vital if we wish to seek the kingdom of God and not merely reinforce our self-delusions.

Starting where we are: fabric and finance

In addition to people and topography, the third element that is vital to understanding the situation of a church is to get a good appreciation of the church buildings and grounds themselves. Only when we are familiar with the condition of our built fabric can we make decisions about prioritizing repairs and maintenance. We can also identify developmental projects that might make an effective missional impact.

For example, Salisbury Cathedral has a robust handle on some aspects of its built environment. The cathedral church itself has been subjected to a major repair programme through which every square inch of external stone and glasswork has been reviewed, and appropriate repairs actioned. Unsurprisingly, this programme has taken forty years. As a result, records and plans of the cathedral are in meticulous order. In other areas, however, data has only more recently given the cathedral chapter a comprehensive overview of its priorities. This includes acquiring Energy Performance Certificates for all our residential properties, plus a systematic condition survey of the public parts of the cathedral precinct (Close). Only when we have a complete overview of our liabilities can we most effectively direct funds where they will have the biggest impact.

The range of reports and advice that a church can get about its buildings is long – and growing. And the data that is received in these reports can be confusing to the general reader. To get a better purchase on this information, it is worth bearing in mind that some reports are statutory requirements, whereas others might be nice to have or relevant only if certain projects are being considered.

Essential documents about Church of England churches and ancillary buildings include:

- The quinquennial inspection (QI). All churches and cathedrals are required to have an inspecting architect or building surveyor who is charged with making a written report at least every five years (more frequently if necessary) on the physical state of the church. This report will identify works required and prioritize them. Are the works needed urgently, within twelve months, one to three years down the line, or further into the future? QI reports come in different styles, but I have always found the most useful to be those which include ballpark estimates of costs.
    - QI reports will also help a church leadership team to understand the history of their built heritage. Not all past construction and modifications have been done well. However, we live in an age which sets far greater store on conservation than previous generations. This means it is essential to know the history of a piece of architecture or object before arguments can be made about retention, conservation, modification or disposal.
    - Free-standing church halls are not required to have a condition survey. However, I have consistently found QIs on halls to be useful for identifying repairs. In the absence of such a report, funds might be misdirected.
- Annual gas safety checks and quinquennial fixed wiring tests (resulting in an Electrical Installation Condition Report: EICR) are requirements for all churches (plus halls and houses owned by churches) that have gas and electrical installations. Annual portable appliance testing (PAT) of electrical equipment that is owned by a church is recommended – but not required. Fire extinguishers

should be serviced every year; further testing is likely to be needed on equipment such as emergency lighting, smoke and carbon monoxide detectors, and first aid kits. Out in the churchyard, checks have to be undertaken on trees, wobbly gravestones, and the condition of pathways (see Chapter 6).
- All buildings that predate the twenty-first century should have an asbestos survey for management purposes. This assessment only needs to be done once, but it forms the basis of an asbestos management file that can be edited if new asbestos-containing materials (ACMs) are discovered or if known ACMs are removed.

In addition to these statutory documents and surveys, there is an endless list of other reports that may be needed depending on the context, condition and proposals for a church, churchyard or ancillary building. Examples are as diverse as access audits, bat surveys, arboriculturists' reports, and so on.

To assist any church through this morass of documentation, expert advice will be needed. Within the Church of England, this will come in the form of your inspecting (quinquennial) architect or building surveyor. Beyond this professional, other specialists might need to be commissioned for one-off pieces of work. And there is a wealth of experience available to parishes through their Diocesan Advisory Committees (DACs). DACs will be considered in greater detail in the next chapter.

Once a church leadership team has a good overview of its people, social setting and buildings, it is in a strong position to plan effectively for the future. In particular, with all this information at its fingertips, a leadership team will be able to determine effectively – and hopefully with a high degree of consensus – which priorities might be agreed for expenditure. It is likely that not all the funds needed for a project of any size will be at the immediate disposal of a church leadership team – Chapter 2 goes into greater detail about funding. Nonetheless, knowledge of people, topography and fabric will help a church to discern what might be done and in which order.

Starting small

Having reflected on the nature and purpose of the church/*ekklêsia*, and the imperative of understanding the situation in which we find ourselves, it remains to say a little about the different scale of building projects that a church might consider. This is because I believe even small projects can have a big impact, especially if such projects can reinforce one another.

Sir Dave Brailsford is a world-leading cycling coach. He led Team Sky to international success in the 2010s. His core philosophy has come to be known as the 'aggregation of marginal gains'. Brailsford argues that small changes may in themselves have only a tiny impact on the performance of an individual or team. However, when combined, the collective effect of small changes can be very considerable. What Brailsford has found to be true of cycles and cyclists, I believe to be true of churches.

Long before I had ever heard of Dave Brailsford, I attended a clergy study day at which the keynote speaker was Baroness Ilora Finlay. She spoke passionately about her opposition to assisted dying from her experience as a palliative care nurse. The core of her argument was that, wherever anyone finds themselves on their end-of-life pathway, there is always something that can be done to make a positive difference. This might be a bowl of fresh soup, a call from a friend, an extra pillow. Finlay was not shying away from the reality or eventual outcome of the process of dying. Rather, she was clear that, even on a path of physical decline, there are small adjustments that can make an immediate, positive effect on the situation of the patient.

Baroness Finlay's words should shape our thinking about buildings management. On hearing her words, I came to realize that what she said about palliative care is equally applicable to any pastoral situation: however dire the circumstances that confront us, and whether the eventual trajectory of an individual or institution is upwards or downwards, there is always something that can be done in the moment to make a marginal difference to improve things. And if this is true of any pastoral situation, then the same might be true of practical problems too, including how Christians manage their buildings: whatever the circumstances that confront us, there is always something that can be done that will make a marginal difference for the better.

Reflecting on the principle of starting out small reinforces a long-standing caution that I have about big projects. When confronted by all the challenges that might face a church leadership team, there are some who will try to solve everything at the same time by sewing up all the fabric issues and opportunities of the church into a major project. This might be about conservation or reordering – or both. There are indeed times when undertaking a big project is the right thing to do. This might be because it is most cost-effective to tackle a number of issues at the same time. Or it might be because the funding streams for the project are best secured as a single lump or within a tight time frame. However, big projects are scary. Sometimes they appear too complex or expensive or time-consuming. If this is the case, the end result is (often) that nothing happens. If you are feeling frightened by the prospect of a big building project, it is worth asking whether you really need it, or whether greater success might be achieved over a longer period by taking things stage by stage. Can you break down the problem and tackle it one piece at a time? Doing things in stages and celebrating small successes can lift the spirits of a congregation that might otherwise feel tired and downcast.

My second caution about big projects is that, once complete, they can be followed by a period of inertia. The church or other commissioning institution can finish the project and then rest on its laurels. This carries the dual risk of not making the best operational use of the project, and of not putting in place an adequate programme of ongoing maintenance. If this is the case, might it not be better to apply the Forth Bridge principle of maintenance (do a little and often), or the Dave Brailsford principle of development, by introducing a continuous cycle of trial, reflection and improvement?

Conclusion

Churches are in the eternity business. We prioritize God and people. But this will probably have implications for our built environment. With both people and buildings, we can only start where we are. And, wherever we start, there are usually some simple things that can be done to make a marginal difference. Having said all this, the reality of God's kingdom is that it never comes in its fullness on earth. This means that there is never a single solution that will fix all our issues in one go. Whether the focus of our individual ministries in the Church is more pastoral or practical (or a combination of the two), our calling as *kuriakos* and *ekklêsia* is to play a part in the continuing life of a process and institution that is so much bigger than the sum of its parts and the span of our days.

2

Preliminaries: Planning, permission, paying, perseverance

Sir Francis Drake knew a thing or two about project management. In the late 1570s, he undertook the second complete circumnavigation of the world in a single ship – and he became the first commander of such a voyage to survive the entire trip. It was an exciting, perilous and costly adventure. Mindful of the enormity of his task, Drake is credited with the following sentiment – words that have been adapted into a prayer, as well as set to music, as in this configuration by Peter Aston:

> There must be a beginning of any great matter, but the continuing unto the end until it be thoroughly finished yields the true glory. The greatest things are accomplished, and the greatest achievements are won, by toil and by striving uninterrupted, toil as well of the body as of the spirit.[1]

Much in Drake's words resonate with any task: the need to integrate theory and practice, body and spirit, and the importance of grit and determination to see things through to a successful completion. With these principles in mind, this chapter seeks to build on the theoretical underpinnings of Chapter 1 by outlining initial steps common to many projects intended to maintain and improve the fabric of our churches, halls and grounds. I say 'many', because not all projects will need to clear all of the hurdles discussed in this chapter. Smaller projects may not need authorization beyond your congregation; some may not even need any funding. However, in the interests of comprehensiveness, this chapter outlines a profusion of plosives: practical preliminaries on which prominent projects are predicated – planning, permission, payment and perseverance.

Planning

Drake's expedition around the world did not happen in a vacuum. Just as the moon landing of 1969 was set against the backdrop of Cold War competition between the United States of America and the Soviet Union, Drake's voyage was part of an English challenge to the dominance of Spain and Portugal on the high seas. Something similar goes on in the background of all successful building projects: they emerge in response to an identified need, which they seek to resolve in ways that fit the vision and resources of the organization. Many blue-sky ideas can be discussed as possibilities but, unless they tackle a specific challenge, they are unlikely to be realized.

We saw in the last chapter how successful churches think strategically about sharing the gospel. This strategy is likely to be laid out in an MAP or similar document. Many MAP goals sketch projects that a church can organize within its existing facilities. For example, it might wish to start a parent and toddler group to strengthen its support for families in the area. Some goals, however, might require physical adaptations to a building in order to facilitate the missional outcomes. For instance, that parent and toddler group is likely to require storage for toys and equipment. Can the church repurpose existing space to achieve this, or does it need to install additional cupboards? New cupboards are likely to be a relatively simple and cheap adaptation. However, what if the room earmarked for the toddler group is currently cold, inaccessible to wheelchairs and buggies, or ill-equipped for serving refreshments? These are all higher bars to clear and likely to demand more significant fabric intervention, be it in a church building or a hall. The works are likely to be costly in terms of time and money. However, improving heating, accessibility and catering features might have wider benefits for the life of that church. For example, installing of a tea point for refreshments could attract other groups to use the space, as well as improve social facilities for a congregation. Thus, resolving one physical issue might advance other aspects of the church's MAP. On the other hand, if the wrong intervention is made, missional opportunities could be closed down. A tea point will be a blessing to a Sunday congregation, but of limited use if the MAP goal is to host major events, such as wedding receptions.

Navigating this morass of opportunity and risk is not easy and cannot be undertaken quickly. A combination of prayerfulness and pragmatism will be required. Getting the MAP strategy right is the place to start. Next comes an assessment of which actions are needed to realize the goals of the MAP. At this stage, if building work is envisaged, the church will have to agree Statements of Significance and Needs.

Statemented

A Statement of Significance is required when changes are proposed to a church that is listed, or to an unlisted church in a conservation area (Walter and Mottram, pp. 223–9). This statement is a summary of the history and features of a building. Its purpose is to allow the church and, in due course, the regulatory authorities to weigh up the potential harm to historic architecture and artefacts against the benefits of making proposed changes.

If your church does not already have a Statement of Significance, gathering the necessary information can take time. However, once produced, this is a document that is relatively easy to adapt for future projects. Your DAC should be able to advise about what to put into the statement and whether it wishes to see it in a particular format. It is also worth asking other nearby churches if they have examples of good practice to share.

A successful Statement of Significance will summarize the story of the church building, contents, churchyard and setting. The first paragraph should outline the key moments in the history of the site. This might progress to a description of the built environment and natural topography of the area, any significant ecology, and the patterns of human use. How does the church fit into its physical setting? Turning towards the building itself, the statement should next describe the layout of the church, comment on its overall condition and the services supplied (water, electricity, and so on). A paragraph might follow on any important fittings and furnishings, for example medieval wall paintings,

Jacobean woodwork, Victorian lighting, organ and bells, and notable portable items such as silverware. The names of significant craftspeople or architects who have worked in or on the church should be recorded. It is helpful to include at least one photo of the interior and another of the exterior. A ground plan is important, if possible showing the age of the various parts of the building and how the church has evolved over the years. A map or aerial photo of the district is also useful. Assuming the building is listed, further information on much of the above can be included by adding the Historic England listing description as an appendix to the statement itself.[2]

Alongside the Statement of Significance, a proposal to make changes to a church will also need a Statement of Needs (Walter and Mottram, pp. 246–9). Whereas a Statement of Significance is a gradually evolving document about each church, the Statement of Needs is specific to each project. The Statement of Needs documents why a proposal has been developed, identifies any harm to historic fabric stemming from the proposal, records mitigations that have been made to minimize that harm, and, ultimately, justifies the project by showing why, on balance, you think the needs outweigh the harm. There is an element of subjectivity here, but it is also a useful reality check. If you reach this point and are starting to feel queasy about what you are proposing, it is likely that the regulatory authorities will feel the same. It might be time to rethink and adapt. If, on the other hand, when you have drafted your statements, you realize that what you are proposing can be achieved with little or no adverse impact on the existing fabric, or are confident that the changes will be really beneficial, then you have good grounds for pursuing the project further.

A Statement of Needs should, first, go into more detail than the Statement of Significance about the human use of the church. How many people live in the parish? What is the pattern of worship and how many people attend? How else is the building used during the week: are there visitors or community hirers? Second, the statement should turn to the needs themselves. What is the general condition of the building? Headlines from the last quinquennial inspection should cover this. What are the specific needs to which the project is responding? Link back here to your MAP and to any wider missional benefits of the proposal. For example, a new lighting scheme might respond to many more needs than replacing broken light bulbs. New lighting is likely to lower your carbon footprint, utility bills and fire risk, as well as spotlight the heritage features of a building, enhance worship through using dimmers and by lighting 'scenes', and future-proof against technological obsolescence. Third, the Statement of Needs should describe the proposals themselves. It might be sufficient here to attach the drawings or scheme of work produced by your architect. Fourth, the statement should relate the two preceding sections (needs and proposals). How does the intended scheme address the needs? You should actively embrace the overt missional benefits of your proposed changes in this section. After all, it is the distinctive requirements of the Church that justify ecclesiastical exemption from the secular planning process (see below pp. 26–7) and the Church permissions process will require you to explain how your proposals will benefit your faith community. Finally, the statement should consider the impacts of the proposals on the heritage of the building and how any harm to the building will be minimized. For instance, with that lighting scheme just discussed, is it possible to avoid screwing into historic fabric by reusing the fittings of the previous scheme, or suspending the fittings in a way that requires no drilling? Inclusion of an options appraisal at this point might be helpful, showing why you prefer one solution to other alternatives.

The Statements of Significance and Needs are corporate documents. Even if they are written by one or two people, they next need to be endorsed by a vote of the PCC.

Building the team

It is unlikely that a PCC will wish to manage a whole project through its regular meetings. This means that, alongside approving the statements, the PCC should also appoint a team to oversee the project, including an appropriate leader. The make-up of the working party should reflect the scale of the project and the skills needed. If small, cheap and straightforward, it could be delegated to one or two members. If large, expensive and complicated, it is probable that more people will be required, as well as skills beyond those of the PCC. There may be some experts within your congregation or wider community who might be persuaded to get involved on a pro bono basis. Even if you are fortunate in this regard, the project team may need to include or receive input from one or more professionals. The obvious voice here will be that of your architect. A PCC is not compelled to use their inspecting (quinquennial) architect to oversee any project on the church. However, more often than not it makes sense to start with this specialist because they will probably know more about the conservation requirements of your building than anyone else. If a church chooses not to use its QI architect to support a particular project, the DAC may ask the PCC to explain why it has appointed an alternative.

Vital though an architect is on any project, it is important for the PCC to keep a close eye on professional costs at this stage. An architect will usually quote fees at an hourly rate or as a percentage of the total cost of a contract; this percentage is often 10 per cent or more, so it can make a big difference to the final bill. Other professionals may also be needed for the planning and delivery if further expertise is needed. It may be a requirement of the planning process to understand the impact of a proposal on local ecology or the structural integrity of a building. Alternatively, it may be a condition of permission granted that an archaeologist has a watching brief over any excavations. Given that a considerable amount of professional input may be required to get a project to the point where it receives permissions to proceed, the PCC should consider the extent to which it is prepared to put assets 'at risk' during the planning phase.

While the PCC as managing trustee has ultimate responsibility for establishing the team to deliver a project, individual members of the PCC will probably ask themselves about the extent to which they wish to become involved. In particular, if you are the vicar or a churchwarden, how much time and energy could or should you commit to the project? You may be hard pressed by other duties. On the other hand, you may think that the success of the project will have such a positive impact on the life of your church and your role within it that you elect to set your shoulder to the effort.

Leading the team

Particular thought should be given to the type of leadership needed for a project. By this I especially mean the extent to which the chair of the working party needs to take an executive role. For example, later in the book I describe a project to install an accessible toilet facility at the smaller church in the parish where I was ministering (pp. 149–53). This was not the largest, most expensive or longest project which I have led; however, it was probably the most demanding in terms of the level of detail that was asked of me as chair. I had to be intimately involved in the production of grant applications. I was later drawn into technical details of construction and invited to meetings to admire different styles of brick, door handles and light switches.

By contrast, I was simultaneously leading a working party of the Governors at the parish primary school. We were looking to expand the school by two classrooms, build ancillary facilities onto two sites, and undertake an extensive renovation of the overall heating system. There were multiple heritage issues (listing, conservation area, scheduled ancient monument, tree protection orders, and so on), and the contract value was ten times that of the church toilet extension. However, I was very grateful that I did not need to be so executive with the school expansion as with the church toilet scheme. The architect led on the process of obtaining planning permission and other consents; school staff and colleagues in the diocesan office dealt with the finance; and construction was overseen by an outstanding local contractor. As chair, I could concentrate on convening and leading the working party, providing occasional support for the headteacher, and – at one crucial juncture – chivvying our professional advisers to ensure that we met vital deadlines in order for the scheme to be delivered on time.

Being involved in these two projects at roughly the same time, I learned that there is not necessarily a direct relationship between the size and cost of a project and the amount of input needed from the team leader. In some ways, smaller projects can be more demanding: the budget may be tighter and there may be fewer people who are willing and able to get involved.

Permissions

Having built a team and agreed a plan, the next challenge is to obtain the necessary permissions. Those who are new to church leadership, lay or ordained, may be taken aback at this point by the apparent complexity of the hoops through which they must now jump to initiate a project. Six denominations (Church of England, Church in Wales, Roman Catholic Church, Methodist Church, United Reformed Church, and member churches of the Baptist Union) have been granted what is known as 'ecclesiastical exemption' from planning laws in England and Wales. This does not mean these Churches can do what they like. Rather, proposals to change the interiors of their places of worship are subject to internal processes within each denomination – and external works still need planning permission, as we will see shortly. Ecclesiastical exemption has been granted on the argument that Churches are best positioned to know what is theologically most appropriate within their liturgical spaces.

Within the Church of England and Church in Wales, local churches need to obtain a permission document called a 'faculty' (although some minor or temporary works may be permitted by a formal letter of consent from an archdeacon). Faculties are issued by a legal officer known as the chancellor of the diocese. Chancellors are senior and busy figures, such as judges – and not to be confused with the chancellor of your cathedral, who is likely to be a priest not a lawyer. The chancellor of the diocese will be advised in making their judgements about the church fabric by another legal officer called the registrar, and also by experts in various forms of conservation who serve on the DAC.

The role of the DAC is vital to the operation of ecclesiastical exemption. Details of the secretary who administers the DAC in your diocese should be available through the diocesan website. Each DAC consists of volunteers who have professional skills in the range of fabric issues that confront churches (structural engineers, organ builders, campanologists, specialist electricians and heating experts, stained-glass conservators, and so on). Formally, their role is to advise the chancellor about which faculties to permit and which to refuse. However, most DAC time is now effectively spent facing in the other direction: advising parishes as they develop proposals. This represents a sea change within the mentality of DACs: away from the role of policeman and towards a positive engagement with parishes to promote the alignment of local church mission and the interests of heritage preservation. This way, hopefully the chancellor can approve most of the applications with which they are presented. Given this, you should regard faculties as a tool for managing change, not for blocking it, and the DAC as a friend, the advice of which should be sought as early as possible. The later a

DAC becomes involved, the greater the risk that conversations may become confrontational rather than constructive.

The DAC will be able to help you to make connections that might not otherwise have been possible, for instance by sharing examples of equivalent projects in other contexts: both what has worked well and what might be best avoided. The DAC will have extensive knowledge of your building and the records of previous applications that may offer a parish leadership team some objective distance on issues and possibilities beyond the sometimes jaded perspective of parish folk memory. In moving beyond their traditional remit, some DACs and diocesan buildings teams are particularly keen to support parishes around the challenges of carbon reduction and opportunities to capitalize on halls assets, as discussed elsewhere in this book.

Some DACs offer training on how they operate or have one or two spaces at each meeting for non-members to observe their discussions. If you are in a position of leadership in a church that might be heading towards a project that will require support from the DAC, I would strongly encourage members of your working party to take advantage of such opportunities.

Having worked with your project team and DAC, you will hopefully arrive at a scheme that can be put before your PCC for approval. With PCC approval in place, the formal application process can begin. This process has increasingly moved online over recent years. The new national portal for DAC applications provides consistency and familiarity across England, but may not be easy for those who are nervous about computers and the Internet.[3]

Once your online application form has been completed, you will need to consult with interested parties. As a minimum, this will involve a notice in the church porch and on your website; this advises that you are seeking a faculty, how the public can view your plans and the contact details of the registrar, should they wish to give a compliment or complain about what is being proposed. There is a 28-day window in which public comments can be received. These may come from those within your congregation or local residents. Sometimes consultees may make a collective response, for example through a residents' association or local amenity society.

Alongside this public consultation, the DAC may ask you to consult with specialist bodies. Some of these are statutory consultees who have a right to be notified of your proposals as they enter the permissions process. Pre-eminent here is Historic England: this is the organization responsible for the national listing of heritage assets. There are also six 'national amenity societies' that may wish to express a view on your project, depending on whether it falls within the remit of their group. The Society for the Protection of Ancient Buildings has a particular interest in the repair of medieval buildings. Similar is the Georgian Group, which covers buildings and landscapes dated 1700–1840; the Victorian Society, which covers 1837–1914; and the Twentieth Century Society, for 1914 onwards. The Council for British Archaeology has a similar role as regards archaeology, as does Historic Buildings and Places in relation to monuments. If you have a well-planned and well-presented case, hopefully these consultees will be in a position to commend your proposals – or merely not to comment.

Work which is undertaken on the outside of the church will be visible to members of the public as well as those who use the church as a place of worship. As a result, exterior works are subject to 'dual control': both a faculty and planning permission are required. If you are in this situation, you will need to run an equivalent application for planning permission (and maybe Listed Building Consent) by your local authority. You should seek advice from your architect about whether it is best to seek planning and faculty approval at the same time or to tackle one process before the other. Much of the paperwork required for the faculty application can be reused for the planning application. However, additional consultees may be drawn into a local-authority planning application, for instance around ecology or drainage.

Nothing is ever simple in the Church of England, so it is worth noting that cathedrals fall outside the faculty system. They have ecclesiastical exemption but, instead of a faculty, they must seek permissions for internal works from bodies known as the Cathedrals Fabric Commission for England (CFCE) and/or each cathedral's own Fabric Advisory Committee. If you find yourself as a trustee (chapter member) of a cathedral, it is worth being genned up on the rules that govern this system. These are the Care of Cathedrals Measure 2011 and the Cathedrals Measure 2021. The Association of English Cathedrals frequently runs helpful training courses for those who are new to cathedrals governance and that explain these Measures. Your cathedral should also have a 'liturgical plan': this describes how you use the building for worship around the year, as well as any proposed developments. The CFCE may ask how some proposed building projects align with your Liturgical Plan, so it is important to be apprised of what is in the document and to ensure it is updated with reference to the sorts of development that you might like to make.

In my experience, most projects that require faculty permission are small and uncontroversial. As such, they receive little or no attention from potential consultees and so are likely to sail through quickly to the point where the chancellor can make a determination. However, consultees can sometimes object to aspects of your proposals. If objections come from one of the statutory consultees, you should get in touch with them and talk through the issues. Sometimes it may just be a matter of providing additional information to show that you have a robust and reasoned plan. Sometimes you may need to make compromises to your scheme in order to ameliorate the consultees' opinion. The faculty and planning processes will set greater or lesser weight on the objections of different consultees, so you may need to think tactically about the organizations you wish to assuage. Most important is Historic England: serious objections from HE are likely to lead to your proposals being refused permission.

If objections come from a non-statutory consultee, you should consider carefully whether you wish to engage with them. With an individual objector (e.g. a householder), it might be possible to reassure them by inviting them to discuss their concerns. For example, a neighbour objected to one project with which I was involved because the scheme involved a change of roof line. Quite reasonably, the neighbour was concerned about the potential loss of light and the adverse impact which this might have on their plans to sell their property. In conversation, we determined that a small reduction in the roof line was sufficient to alleviate the neighbour's worries and persuade them to lift their objection.

However, it may not be possible to get all consultees on board with a proposal. This is especially true if your scheme is opposed by local lobbyists who represent vested interests. Be it covert or acknowledged, heritage preservation can become a convenient veil for protecting private privilege. It is a frustration that such pressure groups can even acquire charitable status – although members of such organizations are at risk under tax law if they fund their charity as a vehicle for pursuing personal interests. The risk from such groups is that they try to manipulate the press or social media. They can also make noise disproportionate to their numbers.

Vexatious campaigning within the permissions process is fortunately rare, although it never hurts to think through some stock responses for print or verbal comment, should they be needed. The good news is that when objectors become actively objectionable, they are likely to overreach and alienate themselves. For example, it is an unwritten rule of the faculty and planning process that comments should be channelled through the registrar or local authority planning officer; direct lobbying of one consultee by another is likely to expose the extremity of a lobbyist's position in the minds of the other consultees whom they are seeking to pressure.

Given the complexities of the checks and balances in the faculty and planning system, it would be unreasonable to claim that the system is perfect or that it always produces the best outcome. I have occasionally seen aspects of the faculty system that seem perverse or unduly procedural. I can think of a church that received a request that it apply for a faculty to remove a tree – several months after that tree had been blown down in a storm. I can think of a churchwarden and vicar who used a faculty to undertake lifting a significant piece of historic stonework in preparation for an assessment leading to a second, more major, application for repairs. During the preparatory work, it was discovered that the internal damage to the stonework was less severe than had been anticipated and that an *in situ* repair could be effected. But this was only possible if undertaken within the few remaining hours that the lifting equipment was on site. The vicar and churchwarden were advised by the DAC that this variation of plan would require a faculty, the acquisition of which would take months. The vicar and churchwarden took the decision to ask for the repair to be completed by the masons who were on site, rather than follow through with the terms of the original faculty to dismantle and remove the stonework from the building. This action would have incurred both extra cost and risk greater damage to the historic fabric of their church. I can think of a church which was applying to turf over a garden of remembrance: an unassuming measure to simplify the management of its grounds. Although the chancellor told the objectors that the PCC owned the land in which the ashes of their loved ones had been buried (unlike a cemetery where plots are leased), he nonetheless eventually ruled against the PCC, seemingly on the grounds that his ruling would be more likely to achieve pastoral reconciliation with those objecting to the scheme. This seemed a strange outcome, given that the objectors who were so hysterical about the land never worshipped in the church and so lacked any Christian theology of death and the hereafter.

Having said all this, the system of planning permission and ecclesiastical exemption is probably the least worst option available. It is a system of consultation and permission that allows a project to be thoroughly scrutinized from all angles so that an informed decision can be made about whether a scheme should go ahead.

Paying

Returning to Francis Drake and the nautical metaphor, there is no doubt that charting a successful course through the permissions system can be an arduous exercise. Alongside this, you face the challenge of paying for your voyage. Even if permission is granted, no vessel should set sail if there are insufficient funds to reach the intended destination. Jesus himself talked about this (see Luke 14.28–30).

Given what we saw about a church venturing funds 'at risk' near the start of a project, it is usually prudent to tackle the question of funding while you are seeking permissions. If you opt to deal with financing and fundraising after a project has permission to proceed, it is likely to delay delivery, risk increasing the cost through inflation, and potentially breach any time limit imposed by the chancellor as a condition of the faculty. Furthermore, the DAC application process will result in scrutiny of the financial viability of a project: the faculty petition form enquires about the cost of the project, what funds the PCC has secured for the works, and what plans are in place for obtaining any shortfall. In addition, the faculty might specify that work should not commence until the chancellor is satisfied that adequate funds are available. This protects against a parish entering into obligations that are beyond its means and, by extension, an unnecessary threat to the payment of that parish's share (quota) to the diocese, or wider reputational risk to the Church as a whole. (Within regard to cathedrals, an equivalent regulatory check is provided by the Church Commissioners, who need to be consulted for high-value property projects in order to ensure that cathedrals maintain their endowed assets for the long term.) All this means that it is usually prudent to progress how you are going to fund your project at the same time as seeking permissions. Inevitably, this means that more time is demanded of the project-delivery team. Depending on the size of these demands, it might make sense to split the working party into financial and operational sections, or to create a parallel group to look at the question of funding.

Finance for church building projects can come from many different sources. The precise mix will depend on the size and nature of a scheme – and sometimes on circumstance and good fortune. At heart, it is a matter of finding out which people or institutions might be interested in your proposals and doing your best to bring them on board. In addition to the examples given in the pages that follow, Chapter 7 is illustrated by two church hall renovations that drew on very different funding streams, notably neither of which required congregational fundraising. These show the crucial principle of a church aligning its goals with those of others in order to achieve a mutually beneficial outcome.

Grants

When thinking about grants there is a tendency for churches to automatically zap to the National Lottery Heritage Fund.[4] After all, the NLHF is the biggest funder of heritage grants in the UK. Under the terms of its post-Covid relaunch, the NLHF has two funds, one making grants of between £10,000 and £250,000, and a second making grants of between £250,000 and £10 million. With both funds, successful bidders will need to show how their project meets each of four criteria to a greater or lesser extent: saving heritage; protecting the environment; inclusion, access and participation; and organizational sustainability. Full details are available on the NLHF website. If you are going for one of their grants, make your pitch wisely. You may only get one shot at it: don't apply in one year if you might have a bigger and worthier project coming down the track shortly afterwards.

But don't just think NLHF. There are thousands of grant-giving bodies in the UK. Some are big, many are small; some national, many local. Some are charities; some are corporate institutions or parts of government. Few are interested in funding projects of a 'religious' nature, but many are prepared to partner with faith groups towards projects with outcomes that are about more than proselytization, especially those that demonstrably press the buttons of equality, diversity and inclusion (EDI), issues on which many churches know they need to do better. EDI can be improved, for example, by increasing access to your historic building, or making your hall more useful to wider sections of the community. There need not be any dissimulation about motivation here because most churches will want to increase the number of people with whom they have contact. After all, such people may, in time, come to be shaped by the ethos and people of a church community.

The age of the Internet should have made it easier to link up grant-making bodies and potential recipients. However, the best search tools are often hidden behind a paywall. To get over this problem, does your diocese (or equivalent regional/national Church body) subscribe to GrantFinder or a similar platform? A previous diocese for which I worked had a Historic Church Buildings Support Officer who had done a lot of the spade work on the search engines already, and they maintained lists of grant-making bodies that were worth approaching, divided by theme (e.g. toilets and kitchens, children's work, stained glass and music). Within these lists, useful annotations were provided about each potential donor. For example, some were only interested in funding projects within a geographical area or on buildings from a particular era. Each funder has its own values and priorities, not to mention its own application form and cycle of meetings around the year. It is important to make a tailored approach to each organization so as to make the strongest positive impression on its trustees. While some generic information from the Statement of Needs may be relevant to all grant-makers, a clumsy cut-and-paste job will reduce your chances of success.

There are some projects for which the list of potential donors is thin and so valued relationships with a few bodies may be even more important. It might be possible to call on funds from these bodies only occasionally, so care and planning is needed to ensure that a precious donor is not tapped for a project that might attract funding from elsewhere. For example, Salisbury Cathedral is particularly grateful for the support of the Friends of Salisbury Cathedral. The cathedral relies on this group for funding towards projects that will not attract grants from other sources. This includes projects of a more overtly religious nature and some that are important but, frankly, unglamorous. Thus in 2022, the Friends generously gave £125,000 towards relamping the exterior of the cathedral with light-emitting diodes (LEDs), slashing utility costs and the carbon footprint. They followed this in 2023 with a £100,000 grant, which paid for a portable dais around the new altar beneath the spire of the cathedral; it helped to realize a decades-long vision for liturgical furniture worthy of such an iconic space. Few other grant-makers would have been interested in these projects; the cathedral is deeply thankful for such Friendliness.

Organizations that make larger grants are likely to wish to develop relationships with you and your project. Given this, it is prudent to identify your priorities and any red lines in advance. Some grant-makers will be looking for shared publicity, either at a launch event or through the reproduction of their logos on your printed or electronic publicity materials. Some will wish to have update reports from you after completion of the project, such as evidence of impact and value for money.

You should also be alert to the source of the funds that may come your way through grants not just from corporate bodies but also from individual donors. Some churches are unwilling to receive money from the National Lottery because their grants come from the proceeds of gambling. Most will want to avoid funds that have been generated through the sale of controversial products, such as fossil fuels and addictive pharmaceuticals. Your church may wish to document some basic principles in this area, in the form of an ethical fundraising policy.

Donations

Donations are another major stream of support for church projects, especially if grants are unforthcoming. For instance, renewing the heating and lighting of a worship space is unlikely to attract the attention of grant-making bodies. It may, however, be of paramount importance to a congregation or local community if they are to maintain a functional church building.

First, if a project is going to be pitched to a local congregation, care needs to be taken about messaging and the project's integration with other asks. I am thinking here in particular about regular faithful giving from the congregation towards ministry costs. It does not make sense for the churchwarden to launch a major building project the week after the treasurer has fronted the annual giving campaign. It is far better to wait until such a time as the big project is likely to land well: for example, during a review of the MAP or the annual meeting when priorities are outlined for the year ahead. Second, in pitching a project to a congregation, there will be a simultaneous need for realism and honesty. There should be realism on the part of the church leadership about the ability of members to contribute, based on their intuitive understanding of incomes and liabilities within the congregation. Balancing this should be honesty as regards the need, levelling with the congregation about the importance of the project: 'You know how much it would cost to replace the boiler or heat pump in your home; we have a bigger bill here in church, but this is how much it will cost if we break it down between us.'

One way in which realistic assessment of a congregation's ability to contribute can be balanced with honesty as regards the urgency of the need is by providing a list of price points for parts of the project. St Michael's, St Albans, had an urgent need to replace its entire heating system in 2014; it was confronted with an unanticipated, unbudgeted six-figure sum. Leaning into this challenge, an entrepreneurial worshipper arranged an ingenious campaign. It listed the important items that we would have to purchase, from pipe clips at £10 each, piping at £100 a metre, fan convectors at £1,000 each, and two boilers at £10,000 each. OK, the sums did not exactly correspond with the cost of the materials and their fitting, but it was simple for the congregation to visualize the need. Everyone felt they could make a difference, while those with roomier pockets were challenged to dig deep. Most of the funds that we needed were received from the congregation and the project was delivered on budget and on time.

The renewal of St Michael's heating is an example of a project that was largely funded through donations from a major appeal. I tend to think that crowdfunding schemes like this are at their most effective when used for large projects, especially when presented (as it was in St Michael's) in a pyramid form. A stunning example of success with this model combined private donations with a wider funding mix to realize the refurbishment of St Mary's, Burry Port, in 2008–11.[5] The price-point model can be used for smaller schemes – e.g. 'sponsor a chair' – but I would caution against using it often so that multiple requests are not being made too frequently of the same pool of donors.

Noting this however, appeals are more likely to raise serious dosh than that other route much beloved of churches – fundraising. Fundraising can be a good community-building exercise but involves a lot of hard work for relatively little return. Endless fetes, sponsored abseiling and Smartie-tube challenges are unlikely to move the dial significantly. Other options should be used first.

It is worth noting as an aside that churches are sometimes offered donations in kind or unsolicited gifts of money for a project that is dear to the heart to the donor. This sometimes happens following the death of a loved one whom a donor wishes to memorialize. Such offers are usually a delight to receive but should be handled carefully. Ideally, donors are open to suggestions as to how the church might use their gift – but sometimes their suggestions are quite specific. Questions should be asked: do we really need that new cabinet, pulpit fall or tea urn? One church I know even had an iron safe given *in memoriam* of a former worshipper; I can only begin to imagine what a stalwart she must have been! The PCC may need to reserve the right to direct a donor towards an alternative project, or – in extreme cases – to say no. I found it helpful in parish ministry to have a list of projects, with various price points, to which I might turn when someone offered to give something for a specific cause or *in memoriam*. This might be another instance when a church would be well served by agreeing a fundraising policy, in this case to stipulate how it would consider specific donations; and also a memorials/monuments policy that sets out whether the church is willing for individual names or good causes to be marked on objects.

Legacies

One specific form of personal donation comes in the form of legacies. Legacies are a huge boon to churches in that they cannot be budgeted for and so arrive as a windfall gain.

Legacies can provide useful funding to underpin building projects. For example, one part of the liturgical furniture at Salisbury Cathedral was purchased through a legacy from a recently departed priest in the congregation. Their legacy had been left without condition but, knowing their spirituality and calling, it seemed fitting to spend it on the new altar for the chapel at the east end of the cathedral.

There is a conversation here between a church's needs and donors' desires. Churches generally prefer legacies to be left without restriction for general purposes, but legators may wish to leave money for an aspect of church life that is important to them. This conversation is best framed after a church has approved a legacy policy. A legacy policy need not be complex but should affirm the desire of the church to receive legacies, and to encourage these to be left for general purposes. Alternatively, the donor could be asked to speak in confidence with the minister or relevant lay officer of the parish if they are thinking about specifying how they would like to restrict their gift. If they do wish to restrict a legacy, how does their proposal sit alongside the known needs of the church? Is it complementary, neutral or even antagonistic to the church's aims?

Once a legacy policy is confirmed, it is possible to integrate information about legacies with the annual giving campaign, thereby encouraging worshippers to consider leaving gifts in their wills. I have found it helpful at this stage to include information about how legacies of different sizes have been used in the past. For example, the St Michael's, St Albans, legacy leaflet noted how one legator left an unrestricted gift in their will and that, after their death, the PCC agreed with their family to spend it on enhancing a section of the churchyard with resin-bonded gravel. These works improved access to the peaceful area where we buried the ashes of the legator; their grandson, a wheelchair user, is now better able to visit this precious and peaceful space.

Messaging is everything. I was amused to hear a priest promote his parish's legacy strategy as 'pray now, pay later'. It is a catchy and memorable phrase. However, on reflection, I don't think it is quite what we want to be saying about legacies. Some worshippers will have assets tied up in property that they cannot immediately realize; but congregations need to hear a message about the present-day life of the Church and costs of ministry – please pay now – in addition to which legacies are a special way of making a lasting contribution when we are praying on another shore – please pay later too.

Inevitably, promoting legacies is a strategy for the long run – a casting of bread on the water. Legacies are unlikely to bring in funding at the time when we really need it. However, they are an important way of being honest with our congregations about the cycle of life and death, and the values that we wish to outlast us. Legacy campaigns sow seeds from which we hope our descendants in the congregation may benefit in years to come. And we are in the eternity business.

Reserves

When all other options have been exhausted, a church will need to consider whether it should spend its reserves – should it be fortunate to have any. At this point, a careful cost-benefit analysis will be needed as a guardrail against two opposite risks. There are those churches that fastidiously cling onto reserves 'for a rainy day'. But what if that day has arrived and the rain is literally coming through the ceiling? In addition, grant-making bodies and donors will be cautious about supporting organizations that hold too much in reserves, preferring to work instead with more deserving and less-cautious cases. Conversely, there are those churches that spend their reserves because it is the easy thing to do, without seriously planning to stabilize a downward trajectory. This pattern might start with a small loss one year that, if not arrested, will grow and grow until the church is bankrupt.

The case for using reserves for a building project needs to be conceived around the potential return on investment. Will the project represent an enhancement to the mission and evangelism of the church? Will it bring in more visitors or community use and so increase the church's income? Will it increase the capital value of the church's assets? Care should be taken when exploring this last point. You should seek advice about what would happen in the event of the church's ever being sold. What proportion of the proceeds would accrue to the local church, or would some be creamed off by the diocese or national structure of your denomination? With all the above questions, how confident does the church leadership feel about the potential missional or financial returns of your project? What metrics might quantify this?

Of course, church assets are not just held in cash or stocks. Sometimes they take the form of property or portable objects. If the church owns a house which is surplus to operational requirements, what are the pros and cons of liquidating this asset to invest in the proposed missional project? Does it make sense to sell the dilapidated parish hall and downsize if the proceeds could be used to transform the interior of the church into a more multi-use community space? A major instance of such a concentration onto one site was completed in 2021 at St Philip and James, Leckhampton, after a period of two decades' gestation.[6] Another example may be found in a radical equity-release scheme at St John's, Radlett. By entering into a partnership with a commercial property developer to build six units of affordable housing, enough surplus was generated to completely demolish a tired post-war church and replace it with a new worship space, plus a separate hall and kitchen for maximum community flexibility around the week. The Rector of Radlett writes that

> so far it's working well – people love the brightness and new-feel, and it has attracted a lot of new groups, who are paying for the utilities. We have a full-time nursery in some of the rooms and a large catering-standard kitchen. So it is still an asset and not yet a liability![7]

A church rebuilt through commercial partnership: St John's, Radlett (2024).

Occasionally, churches that own objects of exceptional value may choose to sell these to fund missional fabric projects. A good example here is Holy Trinity, Bradford-on-Avon.[8] Holy Trinity discovered that it owned a painting called *Christ Blessing* by the old master Quentin Metsys. The sale of the Metsys contributed the bulk of the £2 million in funds that were needed for a substantial internal reordering. The project included an underfloor heating system, kitchen pod, meeting room, additional toilets and various refurbishments, including to the organ.

Many issues were resolved through this project and lots of missional opportunities opened up. I was not party to the conversations but can imagine discussions revolving around whether it was appropriate or possible to house such a valuable painting within the church. And, once the decision to sell it had been taken, what was the most appropriate use of the funds raised? Churches that are in the fortunate position of owning such portable assets of significant value should consider the merits of a collections policy to guide their thinking around potential acquisitions and disposals. And early advice from your insurers about the costs and security implications of retaining objects on site might also shape your thinking.

Christ Blessing: *the painting that launched a transformation in Holy Trinity, Bradford-on-Avon. See the image on p. 78 for a photo of Holy Trinity's kitchen.*

If all else fails, some churches may wish to explore a loan. Not all churches will be permitted to borrow; advice should be sought from your denomination about this. For those that are allowed to borrow, the same rules apply as above, except the stakes are higher: will the building project bring a return on investment that not only repays the loan but also continues to strengthen mission and ministry in a way that bolsters the viability of the church in the long run?

Perseverance: pausing, parking and pressing on

I work for a cathedral that took 38 years to build. Compared to most other great churches of the Middle Ages, this is an incredibly short period of time. However, for those who were immersed in the project, the construction of Salisbury Cathedral was, literally, the work of a lifetime. By coincidence Salisbury Cathedral has just reached the end of a major repair programme that has taken a similar length of time. Some of my amazing colleagues in the works yard have given the whole of their careers to seeing this project through to completion, and to ensure that the cathedral is preserved for many centuries to come. The demands of planning, permissions and payment remind us that some projects take a very long time to realize. Rome wasn't built in a day. We are being recalled to the message of Chapter 1 about long-termism, and the associated need to keep our eyes on the goal. This approach is vital if we are to maintain energy levels and avoid burnout or despondency.

But it is also worth remembering that a particular version of Rome was built. Other options were doubtless considered and rejected for all sorts of reasons (see Colvin). Some buildings are simply unneeded, unaffordable, or not permitted. So, as we consider perseverance in the face of the long slog that is inherent in certain projects, I would advocate three more alliterative P's; these are worth bearing in mind at those moments when essential decisions need to be taken about the direction of a project: pausing, parking and pressing on.

Sometimes we have to be honest and accept the need for a pause. A project might have many laudable outcomes but maybe the timing is not right. Perhaps there are not enough willing hands to form your working party. Perhaps the major grant-making body you were relying on has not supplied the funds. If this is your situation, might God be saying something about his seasons? Might it be that the right thing to do is to rest, regroup and wait for a more opportune moment? In the next chapter, I cite a project that came to an eventual fruitful outcome even though it went down like a lead balloon when first mooted: initially the timing wasn't right; later on it was (pp. 52–3).

Sometimes complications with a project are more than just a matter of timing. Under these circumstances, the project need not be paused but more fundamentally parked. There will always be some ideas that struggle to reach the top of the priority list. We can't do everything and so we must prioritize where we put our money and energy. For example, when I saw the excellent work that had been done in St Andrew's, Bedford, to convert a choir vestry into a multi-use flexible space, I started to wonder why our parish church in St Albans had a choir vestry that was used for only a few hours every week. I began to play fantasy-league architect about what might be done with our equivalent space.

In my mind's eye, I developed the rough idea of turning the back third into a massive walk-in cupboard, where the storage of music and robes could be rationalized; the front two-thirds would be a room where the choir could practise, but free from clutter so that it could be used for church meetings and commercial hire during the week. The project would not have been very expensive, probably costing less than £10,000 to realize. However, it rightly remained parked. This was because, although our choir vestry was hired for a small amount of private music tuition during the week, there was insufficient commercial demand for the space. In addition, the room could only be accessed up a step through a narrow door. And there were no toilets in the building: hirers would have had to make an inconvenient walk across the churchyard to the Parish Centre. Maybe if the commercial demand for the Parish Centre continued to grow it would make commercial sense to look again at a choir vestry conversion.

While some projects are paused and others parked, moments of crisis may arise when the best response is to press on and really go for it. There are times when the project team have to lean emphatically into a scheme if they are going to make it happen. Failure to do so may risk a loss of opportunity.

Two examples spring to mind. During my time as chair of that parish school expansion discussed above (p. 26), there was a pivotal moment when a narrow window to secure funding was about to close. The school governors' working party did not have all the quantifiable information we wanted about demographic trends around local demand for schooling. We were forced to fall back onto intuition and to trust our judgement about the worthiness and potential of the project. We pressed the green button and the scheme went ahead. I have no doubt that it was the right thing to do: the extra classrooms and improved facilities have since played a part in enabling an excellent staff team to expand the pupil roll and raise performance to an Ofsted Outstanding grade (July 2024).[9] Moreover, as a Church school, all this brings more families into the ambit of the parish: the more overtly Christian return on investment that inspired me to back the scheme in the first place.

My second example comes from my current context at Salisbury Cathedral. I was advised in late 2023 by our in-house electrician that he had just bought a lot of light bulbs. 'Fascinating,' I thought. But, our electrician continued, these were very expensive and might be the last batch he would be able to buy. Once this stock was used up, we might have no more bulbs to put into the high-level light fittings in the clerestory and that these fittings were crucial for providing adequate levels of light on the cathedral floor. 'Mmm,' I thought. 'That rather changes matters.' I enquired how long our stock would last. 'About 18 months,' he replied. 'Oh bother,' I thought. The cathedral had known for a long time that there was an opportunity to relamp with LEDs and make big savings on utilities and carbon consumption; but the work had been put off because it could not be phased and would cost a one-off whack of several hundred thousand pounds. However, our electrician's advice made the matter mission critical. Without satisfactory lighting, the whole operation of the cathedral would grind to a halt: no lighting threatened no worshippers, no visitors, no nuffink. With this changed priority scenario, I was delighted that the cathedral chapter shaped its 2024–5 budget to include the relamping and identified two sources of funding. It was definitely another case of when it would have been perilous to pause or park: we had no choice but to press on. Be mindful of such pivot moments when priorities change.

The contents of this chapter represent the hardest stages of any kingdom building project. Getting through the planning and permission phases are often the most time-consuming and energy-draining phases of any scheme. They are not mere preambles. Once permission has been granted, however, assuming funding is in place, the management of construction is relatively straightforward. So let's read on and consider some projects that might make our churches more open and better equipped for mission, before moving on to think about our churchyards and halls as well.

Notes

1 Peter Aston, 1976, 'The true glory'; Sir Franics Drake, 1587.
2 https://historicengland.org.uk/listing/the-list/ (accessed 12.3.25).
3 https://facultyonline.churchofengland.org/home and chelmsford.anglican.org/uploads-new/pages/3a_parish_user_manual_2022.pdf (no longer available).
4 https://www.heritagefund.org.uk (accessed 12.3.25).
5 https://sirgarblog.blogspot.com/2011/11/official-reopening-for-st-marys-church.html (accessed 12.3.25).
6 https://www.churchtimes.co.uk/articles/2021/4-june/comment/opinion/outward-sign-of-the-hope-of-glory (accessed 12.3.25).
7 https://www.stalbansdiocese.org/news/radlett-church-re-opens-after-major-building-project (accessed 12.3.25).
8 https://htboa.org/our-story/restoration (accessed 12.3.25).
9 https://reports.ofsted.gov.uk/provider/21/117451 (accessed 12.3.25).

3

Getting your church open

Churches were built for people because people are the Church. However, too many church buildings give out the opposite message. This is because they are closed. An open church building offers the casual passer-by a place of refreshment and contemplation. An open church says that God might be for you. By contrast, a closed church building conveys a subtle message of disinterest and exclusivity. A closed church says that God is only for those who attend services, that God might not be relevant for the average person on the street.

I have long been passionate about getting churches open. I have seen the difference that an open church building can make to those who are able to enter. I know from first-hand experience how an open church can transform the whole ethos of local Christian communities. This chapter explores the principles behind getting your church open, the practicalities you will probably need to address, and the ways in which you can build on the opportunities created by having a more accessible and welcoming place of prayer. Paul Bond's book *Open for you* is full of wisdom and down-to-earth advice on this subject. However, it is nearly twenty years since he wrote this book, and new opportunities, especially around technology, are now available to open churches, as explored later in this chapter. Much of this will be illustrated by what I saw in St Albans, where the two churches of St Michael's and St Mary's, Childwick Green, began to open their doors throughout the week: they were transformed by the people who came through. The chapter will conclude by considering the related issue of accessibility: how and why churches that are committed to openness need to ensure that their welcome extends to those with additional physical and mental needs.

Why bother?!

There are many reasons why churches do not open their buildings during the week. These merit some reflection: if your church is not currently open and you wish to change things, you will likely come up against one or more of these arguments.

The greatest barrier to opening churches is fear – fear on the part of the congregation about what might happen if their building is open to the public. What if someone comes in who damages the fabric? What if someone comes in with the intention of stealing? What if someone comes in who is homeless? What if someone comes in who is carrying disease or is mentally unstable? What if …? I was once told about a rural church on Anglesey that has been closed literally for decades because older villagers still remembered the day when a sheep once came through the door. Well, so what?!

Sheep aside, the fear that congregations feel about opening their churches is deep-seated and needs challenging. Underlying congregational concerns about opening their church is often a subconscious reluctance to face difference and change. New people represent a threat to the proprietorial ownership that loyal congregations feel towards their buildings. They pour in hours of prayer and maintenance, not to mention thousands of pounds in funding. And, rightly, they regard it as a holy place. As a result, local churches can be intensely treasured by their congregations, some of which like to keep things 'just so'. The upshot of all this is that, while most churches claim that they are welcoming and friendly, the reality is often different. Beneath the superficial message of welcome, the truth is sometimes hedged about with unspoken caveats, in particular the assumption that new people who cross the threshold will think, behave and look like those who are already there – people like us.

Opening a church during the week represents a threat to communities that are trapped in a 'people-like-us' mindset. This is because every new person who comes to a church will add to its story. They will be changed by the experience, but they will also change the place and the people with whom they interact. The poet Neil Powell realized this through a trip to the church at Little Gidding, which taught him that the visitor becomes part of the place, simply by signing the visitor book (Powell, p. 28). Church buildings are intended to incorporate visitors into their own story in the way that Powell identifies. It is part of their *raison d'être* to shape individuals into the building blocks of the kingdom of God. The implication of this is that the fear which besets some congregations about the otherness posed by the outsider needs a gentle but firm challenge. Congregations must be convinced by the reasons for opening their churches, and to have their fears allayed – or at least to have their judgment temporarily suspended. Illustrations from churches that have blazed a trail may help in this regard.

Another reason why some churches might be disinclined to open their doors is local ecclesiology. By this I mean the self-understanding of the congregation about their identity and purpose. Some churches operate a 'territorial' ecclesiology. These are the churches that are embedded in a specific community and understand their mission to be about witness and service to those who live or work in the immediate vicinity. Other churches adopt a more 'gathered' or 'congregational' ecclesiology: they perceive themselves as existing to serve their worshippers, a community drawn from across a wider area by the particular style of worship or teaching in that church.

Churches that operate a congregational ecclesiology may perceive less benefit from opening their doors than those with a territorial mindset. If identity is shaped by gathering a community for prayer and praise, there may seem fewer reasons for opening to locals outside times of worship. It has been a historic strength of the Church of England, as well as a number of other denominations, to operate a parish structure based on the vision of 'a Christian presence in every community'. I am not here criticizing congregationalist ecclesiology *per se*, just a potential effect of it. Although I am a member of a Church that maintains an episcopal hierarchy within a national governance structure, I am mindful of the logic within Protestant thought of why some churches see the fullness of their identity and authority within each congregation. Indeed, even within denominations like mine, which adopt a territorial ecclesiology, a cautious, protective outlook towards church buildings can embed itself within some local worshipping communities.

Those who are opposed to opening their churches, either on grounds of fear or ecclesiology, are likely to express their reluctance in the form of practical concerns. I have sat in church committees where opposition to unstaffed opening has been articulated through any number of arguments about practicalities. Sometimes this is about a lack of personnel: 'We cannot open our church because there is nobody to lock and unlock.' Sometimes the blame can be laid on third parties to whom the church is beholden: 'We cannot open our church because it would invalidate our insurance.' Best of all are familiar tropes about risk: 'We cannot open our church because of health and safety and safeguarding.' Often these arguments are knee-jerk reactions and sometimes they are untrue. As such, they are hurdles that can be overcome, albeit with a modicum of organization and a healthy dose of determination.

Getting ready

Any church wishing to open its doors during the week needs to do so with confidence. This means planning and preparation. It would be counter-productive to open a church that is unsafe or unready to greet the visitor.

The first consideration is to understand the basis on which your insurer will permit your church to be open. Contrary to myth and the expectations of the cautious, it is possible to open your church without personnel on site and with the blessing of your insurance company. Most Church of England buildings are covered by the Ecclesiastical Insurance Group (EIG). EIG has long encouraged churches to be open and unstaffed during the daytime, assuming a risk assessment has been undertaken and mitigations put in place. The reason why EIG takes this stance is because, in their experience, open churches have a lower risk of being damaged or burgled than those that are locked. Their experience says that a thief will be more interested in a building with nobody around than in a building where they might be interrupted at any moment. In the experience of EIG, the best guarantee that a visitor will respect your church and churchyard is the next visitor to come up the path behind them. In addition, churches that have undertaken preparations to open for visitors are likely to be better maintained and so less tempting to those of ill-intent; thought will have gone into lighting, access and grounds maintenance.

EIG thus approves of churches that open on an unstaffed basis during the daytime, after a risk assessment (RA) has been undertaken and mitigations put in place. Churches that are left open overnight do incur higher risks and so face greater premiums. Nonetheless, in some rural areas, that risk might be sufficiently low and manageable so as to not to be unbeneficial. A distinctive example of 24/7 opening will be considered shortly. EIG rightly insists on a preparatory RA. This need not be an onerous exercise. All that is needed is for one or two worshippers to go around the building and assess where problems may occur as a result of the church being unlocked and unstaffed. Usually, it is possible to make simple and effective mitigations of any concerns that are identified.

There are three risks that need to be assessed in an RA for unstaffed opening: theft, malicious damage and arson. If a church is unstaffed, it is prudent to lock away portable objects of value or to protect them by other means. Similarly, any materials or equipment that might increase the likelihood of a visitor causing a fire, either intentionally or by accident, should be removed. Finally, while it is harder to protect against intentional damage, there are measures that could be put in place to disincentivize inappropriate behaviour. Warnings about CCTV are cheap and simple – although take care not to fill your building with angry signage. Better lighting might also reduce any threatening, shady nooks and crannies.

The example RA opposite might give you a few ideas of what to consider in your context. Other templates may be available online or through your insurer.

The RA provides you with a written record of the risk as your team has discerned it, and lists any additional measures put in place to decrease and manage that risk once the church has been opened.

Risk assessment for unstaffed opening						
St Tiddlywinks						
2 March 2024						
A. Rector+						
Mrs C. Warden						
				After controls		
	Risk	**Controls**		Likeli-hood	Sever-ity	Risk rating
C17th chairs	Theft	Chain to pulpit		1	2	2
Altar silver	Theft	Store in vestry		1	2	2
Mics and stands	Theft	Store in vestry		1	1	1
Sound system	Damage	Fix new panel to side of equipment box		1	1	1
Crib figures (January)	Theft	Store in vestry – cardboard alternative during week		2	1	2
Matches	Arson	Store in vestry		1	3	3
Electronic piano	Damage	Store in choir vestry		1	2	2
Historic pulpit	Damage	Pulpit door shut, pull table in front of stairs		2	2	4
Portable pew	Theft	Unlikely – too heavy – no extra controls needed		1	1	1

Likelihood	**Severity**	**Risk rating (L x S)**
1 = Low	1 = Low	1–2 = low priority
2 = Medium	2 = Medium	3–5 = medium priority
3 = High	3 = High	6–9 = high priority

An example of a risk assessment for unstaffed opening.

Worked example: St Michael's, St Albans, and St Mary's, Childwick Green

Making the case

When I arrived as Vicar of St Michael's and St Mary's in 2012, both churches were largely locked outside the hours of public worship. Historic arrangements were in place whereby St Michael's was open during a limited number of summer afternoons, when volunteers were on site. This required a large team of people. There was also a complicated system of access and closure: a key had to be collected by the volunteers from an adjacent museum. Intermittent sickness and family commitments meant that it was not possible to guarantee that helpers would always be available. This meant it was nigh-on impossible to publicize when the church would be open. Inevitably, this led to frustrated visitors and inconvenient knocks on the vicarage door from those who just wanted to look around an interesting and ancient building.

Problems were compounded by a declining pool of volunteers: while those who helped to open and staff the church were enthusiastic, friendly and knowledgeable, the numbers available each summer seemed to be getting fewer. We were going backwards; the church was becoming increasingly less accessible to the casual passer-by.

Perhaps most revealing was that members of the team who were responsible for opening and closing the church laboured under the historic title of 'Church Watchers'. This spoke volumes about the intentions with which the scheme had originally been created. Church Watchers were once recruited to police rather than permit, to protect more than to share.

Despite this unpromising backdrop, it was clear to me that there was a strong case for opening St Michael's on an unstaffed basis. The church is adjacent to a large public park and famous Roman ruins. Hundreds flock to the nearby museum and pubs, especially in the summer months. Each day, dozens walk or cycle through the churchyard, en route to work, the station or local schools.

Given this and my experience of open churches elsewhere, fairly soon after starting in the parish, I mooted the possibility of unstaffed opening. The idea was greeted with a decided coolness. The forces of fear and conservatism made themselves known. Familiar lines were rolled out about its being too risky. I decided that it was better to bide my time and form a plan.

I began by gathering evidence of need. During the summer of 2013, more than 500 of our 'Visitor and Pilgrim' leaflets were taken from inside the church porch. This suggested that literally hundreds of people had reached the porch, tried the door handle, and been frustrated.

But evidence alone was not enough. This demonstrable demand to get into the church had to be combined with a moment of crisis that would alter hearts and minds within the church leadership about unstaffed opening. That moment came when I was approached by the head teacher of the adjacent primary school. She was grappling with pastoral issues in the staff team. Could I help? I wanted to say yes. In particular, I wanted to say that, in addition to my being available to support with a listening ear, there was a nice open church next door where staff could take time out should they need peace and reflection. Except our church was locked.

The acute need in the school was sufficient for me to revisit the matter with the church leadership team and to argue for a trial period of unstaffed opening. To my delight, my colleagues now agreed. Protocols were written for those who were unlocking and locking the church at the beginning and end of the day. And the requisite RA was undertaken. On the back of this, silver candlesticks were safely stowed away when not needed during worship. Clutter was removed to make the place look more inviting.

I was thrilled by the ease with which we were able to implement these preliminary changes – although I am mindful that the removal of what I consider clutter is not always without controversy. In this regard, Nigel Walter observes the difference between genuine gifts and transactions – objects that have been gifted with implicit strings attached. Gifts that are not really gifts can lead to long-standing emotional barriers that churches must overcome if they are to tidy away or even dispose of items surplus to requirements (Walter, 2014, p. 10).

Despite all the preparations, it was not without trepidation that I left the building unguarded for the first time in March 2015. I needed the trial to work so that I didn't have to eat my words and reverse the plan. Fortunately, the experiment proved a success. Within a month, we knew that we would never go back to a locked church.

Securing the experiment

A crude metric of success presented itself in the form of an immediate uplift of cash in the donations box. This was despite the donations box being a profoundly uninviting black metal safe-like structure strapped to the top of a pew. We weren't opening the church for the money, but I knew that once the treasurer could identify the benefits of unstaffed opening and advise the PCC that we were generating new income, we would be on to a winner.

A more qualitative measure of impact came from comments left in the visitors' book. This was deliberately located just inside the entrance door. Visitors also wrote some very moving requests for prayer. By mid May 2015, we had had more than fifty entries in the visitors' book and at least a dozen requests for prayer. I shared some of these at a meeting of the PCC and with the congregation in a sermon. My message was helpfully reinforced when one of our younger adults wrote up some of the comments in a supportive piece in the parish magazine.

Unsurprisingly, prayers were offered for loved ones, living and departed, and for wider global concerns:

- *For Robin, terminally ill.*
- *For Lisa, always in our thoughts.*
- *Peace on earth – thank you.*

Here were people, carrying significant emotional and spiritual burdens, who had found a chance to hand them over to God.

The visitor book was even more revealing. It showed that, in the course of two short months (well outside the main tourist season), St Michael's had been visited by people from across Britain and around the world. This included at least three Australians, eleven Americans, two Canadians, a German, an Italian, a Norwegian, a Romanian and a Tanzanian. Their comments were illuminating. A few described their encounter with the building and the quality of its upkeep:

- *Beautiful church.*
- *An impressive well-kept and cared-for church.*

However, comments about the built heritage of the church were relatively few. To my delight and surprise, by far the largest contingent were expressions of thanks for the spirituality that visitors encountered in the building:

- *Paradise regained – with gratitude.*
- *Trying to understand life.*
- *Some peace from the road (passing truck driver).*

Here was *prima facie* evidence for why we needed to be doing this: the open building was allowing a wide range of people to stumble afresh over the things of God.

Of course, it was not all plain sailing. For years, my bishop had been encouraging greater access to the churches of his diocese. But when I told him that we were going to experiment with unstaffed opening, his immediate reply was, 'Plan for when something goes wrong.' It was wise advice. An early example of the unexpected came in May 2015 when someone called Luis signed his name in the visitors book before writing that 'being gay is cool'. 'OK,' I thought. 'A somewhat unexpected reaction to encountering a tenth-century place of worship. But whatever's right for you, Luis.' Trouble arrived the day after, however, when the next visitor scribbled out Luis' comment, signed the visitors book from 'Adolf Hitler' and then announced that 'Christians are the best people – Muslims out'.

This sort of low-level aggression is inevitable when we engage the craziness of real people. Unpleasant though it was, it was an isolated irritant that could be balanced against the overwhelming evidence of benefit that visitors were receiving from the open church. It allowed us to agree that our basic response to any such problem would be to review and make adjustments so that we could continue to be open. Thus the script of the pseudonymous commentator was covered up and the church remained available to all, gay and straight, Christian and Muslim.

A rather bigger challenge presented itself a year or two later. The imperious cast-iron safe into which cash had once been secreted had been replaced with a more inviting wood and perspex donations tower. This box was far more obvious to potential donors as they left the church. As a result, it attracted more donations. However, the sight of the notes and coins at the bottom also caught the eye of a local criminal, with a track record for stealing from churches. He took a hammer to the perspex lid and stole the cash – perhaps £50 in all. Damage and theft aside, I feared there would be repercussions from those who had been reluctant to allow unstaffed opening: hadn't they been proved right about the risks? To my surprise and relief, the leadership team did not insist on locking the doors again. Rather, they advocated CCTV so that we could keep the building open. They did this because they could see the benefits flowing from having the church open.

Related opportunities

Unstaffed opening was not an isolated project in St Michael's. It resonated with a priority in our MAP about welcome. By considering the two issues in tandem, we could reinforce our impact in both spheres. And so, over the years that followed, a small team worked on simple ways in which we might improve the engagement of our open church with weekday visitors as part of our wider commitment to being more welcoming.

It was obvious that we needed to work on the physical approach to the building and the entrance porch. The welcome team walked the route into the church and tried to imagine that we were doing this for the first time (Walter, 2014, p. 8). How did it feel? What might we see if we came at it with fresh eyes? First, our attention was drawn to the imposing set of gates on the outside of the porch. Few things are less inviting than a closed gate. (Nigel Walter describes well how such physical and figurative thresholds guard many churches: Walter, 2011, p. 20.) Fortunately, the gates could be lifted off the hinges and put into storage. Next, we saw that the porch contained a noticeboard plastered with information comprehensible only to the initiated: screed about finance, regulations regarding gravestones, and the Table of Kindred and Affinity – a snappy reminder in Shakespearean English about who could marry whom. All this verbiage was binned; in its place we mounted a simple colourful poster. The poster showed pictures of people – crucially including children – as well as brief warm words of welcome and the time of the main Sunday service. We were determined that the poster should be about people and not the building. It needed to convey something of the ethos of the place. If someone arrived in the evening and the building was locked, a QR code directed them to the parish website where they could take a digital tour of the interior. This was something that we had arranged to be filmed in return for a modest fee by a cameraman who was recommended by the diocese.

Nothing says welcome quite like the Ecclesiastical Courts Jurisdiction Act 1860.

Next, my team of reviewers went inside. Oh dear. There was a bottleneck of furniture around the doorway that made it uncomfortable to get into the main body of the church. Then there was the side chapel stacked with junk. And at the back of the north aisle was a ladder, threatening to fall on anyone who might graze against it.

We set about making changes. The area around the door was pared back to create a less intimidating pinch point. A banner was professionally designed and mounted opposite the entrance to give a simple inviting welcome to those who came over the threshold. It displayed the church logo plus some of our core values. An attractive leaflet rack was installed on the table alongside the visitors' book. I was clear that the information available from this rack should be focused and attractive. Adverts for yoga classes and third-party concerts were not allowed. What we did display was a notice sheet with details of forthcoming services and events, plus a basic guide for visitors. The aim of this guide was not to offer a dry history of the building but to articulate the living role that the artefacts and architecture play in sharing the Christian story. Thus the first item in the leaflet did not describe 'a fifteenth century font of Totternhoe stone' but was an explanation that the font is where Christians celebrate baptism, the symbolic ritual of entry into the church; it explained why the font is near the entrance door – that it is an invitation to thank God for making us.

Building on this and mindful that the church was attracting international visitors, I posed a 'Pentecost challenge' to the congregation: during a sermon on Whitsunday, I asked those who were fluent in more than one language to translate the visitor leaflet. Within six months, we had ten translations. All the translations proved popular, although they were not used in the ratios I might have expected. Few copies of the German leaflet were ever taken: our German visitors probably spoke better English than most British people. By contrast, the most popular international leaflet was, surprisingly, the Slovak translation. It was a revealing insight into who was coming to the church, even when we did not meet most of them in person.

So much for the entrance. We also set about removing that clutter. The side chapel that looked like a furniture store was turned into a focused space for private prayer. Seasonal prayer cards and other resources were added. A worshipper kindly donated an icon in memory of a loved one.

This quieter side chapel was also an ideal place for installing a votive stand, where people could express their prayers through lighting a candle or writing intentions to be shared during times of public worship. Naked flames in an unstaffed church?! Here was another red flag for the cautious. Once again, however, the insurers came to our rescue. EIG will permit the use of votive stands with naked flames so long as an independent source of ignition is not left nearby. EIG deem matches or lighters to be a higher threat of arson than candles; this is because candles readily blow out as soon as they are lifted, whereas matches can be transported and used elsewhere. EIG also asked that no combustible materials be left near the candles, such as loose papers. This made perfect sense and was easy to implement.

Getting things right for children was another priority. We were fortunate to have a retired teacher of special needs as our enthusiastic parish Welcome Coordinator. Sue set to work clearing out the disused corner where that ladder had once stood, turning it into a special area dedicated for children. A small amount of money was allocated to pay for play mats and soft toys (not noisy ones). The aim was to engage rather than entertain, so Sue also acquired a selection of written materials: some overtly Christian, some not. Several of these books were chosen to explain the rituals of communion and baptism as the services progressed (Murrie, 2010a and 2010b); these proved at least as popular with parents as with the children they had in tow.

Sue was careful to select material for the children's corner that would engage boys as well as girls. It included a range of items that would interest a broad age spectrum, from nursery to the top of primary school. She insisted that the material include a diversity of faces and skin colours among the dolls and pictures of people represented.

The usefulness of the children's corner exceeded our expectations. Although it had been designed for families who did not attend children's church groups on Sundays, during the week I would often find parents, grandparents, or childminders in the corner, sitting with their pre-schoolers, reading the books or playing with the toys.

As time went by, we made a number of further investments in the building that we were confident would benefit visitors and so might ultimately pay for their own installation. Some of these were made in response to visitors' comments or known needs. For example, a group of environmentally minded German visitors left constructive feedback about our lights blazing away when they had come into the church. Little did they know that St Michael's had recently been relamped with LEDs (see pp. 104–5) that consumed very little electricity to run. Nonetheless, they made a valid point about the perception caused by the lights being on. And so we installed a movement sensor that turned the lights off if no movement was detected after a ten-minute period. Even with the low consumption LEDs, we reckoned that this passive infrared (PIR) sensor saved about £1 of electricity a day, and so paid for its installation within a year or two. This also meant that when the church was next visited by a bunch of environmentally minded Germans, they thought that the lights had come on especially for them. Wherever possible, making provision for lighting within an open church is important. Nigel Walter notes the irony of those church entrances that give an experience of being pushed into darkness rather than drawn into God's light (Walter, 2011, p. 8).

Another important investment was a bank card reader. Given the general decline in the use of cash, we knew that it was important to supplement the ways in which the congregation and visitors could support our work. This situation became acute during the coronavirus pandemic, when the use of cash took a further nosedive. One of the problems we faced was that, for good technical reasons, St Michael's had no wifi – and it was going to be hard to install. Fortunately, some card readers can operate on 4G, regularly updating banks via satellite about donations received. The device that we chose was not the cheapest: in addition to circumventing the lack of wifi, we also wanted a reader that was visible to visitors and intuitive for them to use in an unstaffed building, as well as one equipped with a discreet but sturdy security cord. Fortunately, the Church of England's bulk buying service[1] came up trumps and we found the right device for our needs. Purchase and installation cost just under £500. The device was installed in the summer of 2020. We doubted the device would receive much early use because of the lockdown restrictions. Nonetheless, it raised £2,000 in its first year, paying for itself several times over. Importantly, this was new money: there was not a corresponding drop-off in giving by other means.

As an aside on card readers, several Church of England dioceses are offering free or discounted card readers to their parishes. But it is also worth weighing up the various options: some are small and not very user-friendly, whereas others have a more prominent and inviting appearance. The best devices are equipped with touch screens that facilitate variable donation sizes, collect data for gift-aid purposes, and may even integrate with email or other marketing databases.

Lack of helpers?

When our other church got wind of these changes at St Michael's, eyebrows started to rise. St Mary's committee voted to open their church and to make adaptations to become more welcoming. They bought a welcome banner, printed visitor leaflets, and introduced a small wooden tree on which visitors could hang requests for prayer. When it came to dogs, St Mary's was determined to go further. St Michael's felt that it could only permit assistance dogs inside the building, given the interests of other users: especially because children played on the floor. The risks were balanced differently in St Mary's; there was also a devoted dog-lover in the congregation who regularly made sure that there was a bowl of welcoming water available for four-legged visitors.

However, there was a problem at St Mary's. This church has a much smaller congregation than St Michael's, and most live at a distance. This meant the church could roster people only for opening and closing on Saturdays and Sundays. To overcome this hurdle, we came up with the idea of an electronic door opener. This pings the door open at 9 a.m. and locks it again at 5 p.m. A green door-release button ensures that nobody gets stuck overnight if they unwittingly enter at 4.59 p.m. The essential components needed to install this device are a self-closer on the door, an electromagnetic lock, a timer, and a decent locksmith. Installation cost a little more than £1,000, a sum that was paid within a year by new donations from visitors, who were delighted to find that the village church was open at last.

Installation of the electronic door opener did require careful consultation with our insurers. EIG said that, from an insurance point of view, the device would leave St Mary's open 24/7. This was because, if the device were to fail, it would fail leaving the door open so that there would be no risk of anyone getting stuck in the building. However, given that we knew the electronic door opener would, when working normally, secure the building overnight and that EIG were asking only for a 4 per cent increase in the insurance premium, this change was a risk we were prepared to take.

Electronic door openers like this strike me as a no-brainer for many smaller churches. However, to the best of my knowledge, St Mary's, Childwick Green, is still the only example in the diocese of St Albans. Are there any similar devices in churches near you? Might one be a blessing in your context?

Ripple effects

Opening St Michael's and St Mary's to weekday visitors generated lots of qualitative feedback, some of which I documented above. Getting a sense of actual numbers proved more difficult. I did look into buying an infra-red counter that would have registered every time someone went through the church porch, but the price tag was too high. My hunch is that, in the early years of unstaffed opening, weekday users of St Michael's numbered in the region of 5,000 a year, but that this figure grew to nearer 10,000 p.a. by the time I left the parish in 2022. These may seem large numbers. However, broken down, they represent just 15–30 people a day. Numbers at St Mary's were harder to assess but it attracted perhaps 1,000 to 2,000 a year. Even a handful every day adds up. For the purposes of comparison, a professionally staffed and well-advertised local museum in the centre of St Albans reckoned, at that time, that it was attracting only 8,000 visitors a year.

In conclusion, in addition to the many positives of opening the churches outlined above, we saw three other, more covert benefits. These benefits were all longer-term paybacks, but ultimately were of the greatest significance for kingdom building.

First, we discovered that opening the churches drew in new worshippers. A number of those who joined the congregations of both St Michael's and St Mary's recounted that an important part of their journey was being able to access our open churches. The benefit of an open church on congregational growth was particularly noticeable at St Mary's as we emerged from the punitive coronavirus restrictions of 2020–1: with St Mary's smaller congregational base than St Michael's, it only took a few newcomers to have a noticeable impact on the number of worshippers.

I was thrilled but unsurprised by the direct line that could be drawn from unstaffed opening to new worshippers. However, there was a corollary of this process that I had not anticipated, namely that opening the churches also transformed those who were already worshippers. As established worshippers came to appreciate that visitors were enjoying their church buildings, they became less fearful of strangers, and more open to change and newness. I sensed that this was particularly true at St Mary's. Through the introduction of unstaffed opening, key individuals grew in confidence and warmed to the prospect of taking new and reasonable risks for the gospel. Here was an outworking of the principle that every new person who joins a church will shape it as well as be shaped by it.

The third benefit of unstaffed opening at St Michael's and St Mary's was that it had a ripple effect on nearby churches. I have long advocated the magpie principle of stealing good ideas from others rather than reinventing the wheel. At least five other churches heard about our unstaffed opening and got in touch to see whether there was any learning that could be applied in their context, and at least two of these moved to introduce unstaffed opening.

In tandem with this collaboration, the four medieval churches of St Albans joined forces to produce a pilgrim trail for walkers. This project aligned with the ambitions of the local council to encourage visitors beyond the central shopping area and into the wider environs of the city.[2]

Simple and inviting.

Access

Open churches have huge missional potential. However, the built fabric of many churches presents physical and emotional barriers to those with access needs. This is particularly the case in churches that were built before the era of modern materials. Heritage buildings are expensive to adapt and permissions are not always forthcoming. The final section of this chapter therefore offers an overview of the issue of access and briefly explores the ways in which church leaders can engage with it.

Churches are under a legal obligation through the Equality Act (2010)[3] to make reasonable adjustments so as not to discriminate against individuals or groups on the grounds of physical or mental health. This applies not only to acts of worship; it is also likely to pose some particular challenges for churches that open on an unstaffed basis because visitors will need to navigate their sites without assistance from people in the church team.

The most obvious access issues revolve around physical mobility. Many churches in Britain were designed before the age of the wheelchair and often make little or no compromise even for those who use sticks or walking frames. Stone steps are a particular challenge. Some churches are built on hillsides. Others have elevated areas designed to emphasize the theological significance of preaching and/or the sacraments. Imposing sanctuaries may facilitate awe-inspiring liturgy, but they can also make it tricky for worshippers to receive communion. Sanctuaries with many steps will be even trickier for clergy or servers who have mobility issues.

But steps are just the beginning when it comes to mobility. What is the state of the pathways inside or outside your church? Are the aisles and pathways free from hazards that might impede rapid and safe exit in the event of an emergency? Are there armrests on chairs or other means by which those with weak legs can pull themselves up without toppling themselves or the furniture? Are displays and information racks accessible from the height of a wheelchair? Are there places for wheelchair users to sit during worship where they do not feel either hidden or overly visible? This is a particular challenge for churches with a large number of fixed pews because there is a risk that wheelchair users and those accompanying them either get shoved at the back, where they cannot see, or exposed at the front, where they feel incongruous. Consideration should be given, when possible, to creating breaks in fixed seating where those in wheelchairs may be comfortably integrated into the wider congregation.

Just as mobility is about so much more than steps, access is about so much more than mobility. Visual impairment is another significant issue. Are the levels of light in a building high enough for people to move around safely? Is there enough illumination in the seating area and at the lectern for reading service booklets and Bibles? Have all trip hazards been removed, roped off, or otherwise made more obvious? Highlighting edges in contrasting colours may be a helpful mitigation for potentially deceptive changes in height, such as on steps and seats (including toilet seats). Are written materials available in a large print format? Technology may assist here because, increasingly, worshippers and visitors can access written materials online, through a QR code, which they can then adjust on their tablet to a size of font and light contrast that is appropriate for their needs.

And then there is the hoary issue of hearing. Most churches are unlikely to need to provide in British Sign Language, except maybe at large or special services and events. But has sound amplification been installed to improve audibility? All but the smallest of churches now have a PA system. Often these include a loop for those with hearing amplification.

Hearing is a good example of where access sometimes requires a 360 review to identify the issue and a team effort to resolve it. The most frequent complaint I receive after services is from those who say that they could not hear what was being said. There is often an implicit assumption behind such comments that I was not speaking loudly enough. My response is always to thank the person for their feedback and to remind them that there are three aspects to the process of hearing: input, throughput and output. I then advise that I will check with one or two others to determine whether they could hear adequately. If the answer is no, I may need to modulate my voice (the input), or there may be a fault with the sound system (the throughput). However, if the answer is yes, failure to hear the spoken word or music in church is likely to be an issue of output. Was the person really listening? Do they need to adjust their hearing device, if they use one? Diplomacy may be needed to hand the complaint back to the complainant.

The example of hearing impairments also reminds us that not all access issues are visible. Society is increasingly aware of neurodiversity. A particular example springs to mind of a family whose child was diagnosed with an autistic condition; he found social interaction very challenging. Often the boy would become anxious or angry. In this case, the church worked with the family to signpost them to acts of worship that were quieter and shorter, and to encourage them to use a side chapel where their son could have more space, where the family could still feel involved in the service, but where they did not feel exposed should he become distressed.

Access cuts across the whole swathe of church operations, buildings and grounds. Certain areas of the building may need particular attention: toilets for instance. Consideration may need to be given to issues such as the size and directionality of doors, handrails, locks, and the type and positioning of handbasins, driers, paper holders, emergency cords and the rest.

Access is such a vast issue that this brief section of a chapter can do no more than list the headline issues. By its very nature, it is also a topic that will have unique implications for every church building; bespoke consideration must be taken in each context.

It would be easy to become overwhelmed by the access agenda. I suggest three remedies for this risk.

First and most important is the test of reasonability. Which adaptations can realistically be made in a given context in response to the known and anticipated accessibility needs of users? Reasonability is vital because it gives perspective on what is practically and financially possible. However, it must never be used as an excuse for inertia. One example of reasonable adjustment might be the diocese that encouraged each multi-church benefice to target one church within the group that could most readily be adapted for use by those with mobility and visual impairments.

Second, mindful of the adage that the only way to eat an elephant is one mouthful at a time, it may help to chop up the elephant. By this I mean that the issues and recommendations will need to be prioritized, probably over a long period of time. And are there ways of ensuring it does not become a burden or worry for just one member of your leadership team? For example, can you integrate your action plan into the church's normal ways of operating?

Finally, when considering issues of access in a church, it might be useful to ask whether external advice is needed. Maybe the church is relatively small and/or has skills within the congregation to make an internal assessment of the church's requirements. If this is not the case, there are companies that specialize in advising about access. Professional wisdom usually comes at a cost, but this could be avoided if free advice can be had from a church's inspecting architect or insurance assessor. Anglican churches should also consider contacting their DAC, which may have members or contacts with particular insight into access issues. And do ask your DAC about funds: some dioceses have catalysed thinking within parishes about these issues; they make money available to assist with the costs of accessibility audits.

Accessing a cathedral

My experience of access in Salisbury Cathedral is a good illustration of the principles outlined above. Given the size of this massive church, and its grounds and ancillary buildings, we commissioned an access review from a professional in 2023. The adviser undertook a site visit over a number of days and issued a written report several weeks later. The good thing about the report is that it is comprehensive – it covers all the issues and will be valid for at least the next decade. Nothing can now be forgotten. The scary thing is that the report is 120 pages long and has 131 separate recommendations. Having received this professional advice, it was decided at the cathedral executive meeting that we manage the challenge by breaking down the recommendations across seven different areas of our operation. As a result, some issues will be overseen when upgrades are made around the cathedral and precincts; others will be incorporated into the work of our visitor team.

Within these breakdowns of the access report, further divisions have been made into what is possible in the short, medium and long term: some adaptations are easy wins and cheap to implement; others will take longer and need integrating into forthcoming repairs and maintenance. For example, the north porch at Salisbury Cathedral is notoriously awkward: it is poorly lit and has uneven steps at either end; and it contains a gloomy late Victorian wooden booth, with self-closing doors that are unnavigable and liable to trap the fingers or slap the face of the uninitiated. Beyond the items in the access review that we think can be resolved in the long term are those recommendations which we doubt meet the test of reasonability. These are recommendations that represent too high a financial cost or that can only be effected through unjustifiably high intervention in the heritage of the cathedral.

In breaking down the access review in this way, we have prevented the issue of access becoming just another 'thing' to weigh down a member of staff or volunteer. We have also avoided the risk that recommendations are shelved and overlooked. Our eventual goal is for considerations of access to become as naturally integrated into our established ways of working as health and safety and safeguarding. Access needs to be seen as just part of how we do Church well. It is a legal requirement and, even more importantly, it is an expression of how we demonstrate the love of God through the quality of our welcome to everyone.

Conclusion

Open and accessible churches are about so much more than bricks and mortar. They are about the invisible threshold forces that surround places and people, and which have the potential to exclude outsiders. Getting churches open and making them accessible embodies how the buildings of the kingdom help to build the kingdom.

The late-seventeenth-century Bishop Thomas Ken prayed:

> O God, make the door of this house wide enough
> to receive all who need human love and fellowship, and a heavenly Father's care;
> and narrow enough to shut out all envy, pride and hate.
> Make its threshold smooth enough to be no stumbling-block to children,
> nor to straying feet,
> but rugged enough to turn back the tempter's power:
> make it a gateway to thine eternal kingdom.

Centuries earlier, the psalmist said that 'the LORD will keep your going out and your coming in' (Ps. 121.8). The words of Thomas Ken and the psalmist are as relevant today as when they were first written. With a little appropriate interpretation, church buildings can speak eloquently of the things of God. There is something of divine grace in this. The gospel grows by its very nature (Mark 4.1–20). People are not saved by their own efforts, and sometimes the best thing that Christians can do is stand back and give God the room to transform hearts and minds.

Notes

1 https://parishbuying.org.uk (accessed 12.3.25).

2 https://www.enjoystalbans.com/wp-content/uploads/2019/07/PilgrimChurchesLeaflet.pdf (accessed 12.3.25).

3 The Disability Discrimination Act 1995 was repealed in England, Scotland and Wales in 2010, and replaced by the Equality Act 2010, which broadened the scope of protection to include other protected characteristics, such as age, gender, religion, and sexual orientation. The Disability Discrimination Act 1995 remains in Northern Ireland.

4

Projects that make a difference

This is a chapter about specific interventions in your church building that can move the missional dial. It is not about repairs and maintenance – all buildings need to be wind- and weather-tight, with functioning roofs and dry walls. Rather, we will be looking at substantial works, sometimes in partnership with other bodies, that can make your church building more useful across the seven days of the week. In addition, many of the projects discussed here will need careful step-by-step planning and delivery, with the support of expertise from your Diocesan Advisory Committee (DAC) and professional advisers. And because this book cannot serve as a Haynes Manual for every detail of church maintenance or project management, we will be moving rapidly over key issues, ideas and examples.

Inevitably we will see some overlap with other chapters. Some of what we consider here will crop up again when we think about church halls (Chapter 7), and some will touch on measures taken to reduce carbon consumption (Chapter 5). However, if you have jumped here straight from the contents page, thinking that it might provide a shortcut to the solution you need, please go back and read the earlier chapters! Any substantial intervention in your building should only be undertaken after a thorough consideration of your ecclesiology, understanding of your local mission context (Chapter 1), not to mention a process of prayerful planning (Chapter 2). Furthermore, it is essential for churches to review and improve their welcome (Chapter 3) before they consider making any big investment in their buildings. This is because the Church is people first and buildings second. Churches need to embed good practice in ministry first. Any detached jump to refurbishments in the hope that bricks and mortar alone will improve a situation is unlikely to succeed. Churches that try to leapfrog the fundamentals are likely to make suboptimal adaptations to their buildings. I can think of churches in which liturgical reordering or installation of various amenities has been undertaken, but which still lack the congregational cohesion and commitment to make the most of their new facilities when new people start to come through their doors. In addition, getting the stuff about people right will probably be cheaper and quicker than the projects considered in this chapter: the effort you put into people is a potential gift of time and energy that can help you to discern the changes you really want to make to the fabric of your building.

My wife and I have a magnet on our fridge that gently teases the overly simplistic messaging sometimes associated with wellbeing. It reads: 'Never forget you are unique. Just like everyone else.' Churches are no different. They really are unique, each one a distinct building, set in its own social and physical topography. But churches also have traits in common, again human and physical. This allows us crudely to divide the issues of this chapter into two. If your church is a heritage building in which it will be challenging to make drastic alterations, and/or if your church has potential to attract a reasonable footfall of weekday visitors, the adaptations for your context are more likely to fall within the first half of this chapter: glazed porches, toilets and catering facilities. If, on the other hand, your building is of a lower heritage value (as assessed by objective criteria, however much it is cherished by your congregation) or has less potential for weekday visitors and private prayer, then it may have the potential to be enhanced by projects outlined in the second half of this chapter: office space, cafés and shops. These latter works will probably represent substantial interventions in the fabric of your church and may require a long-term commercial partnership. It is not that one path is right and the other wrong, one cautious and the other radical. All interventions have the potential to bring new life, people and finance within the ambit of your congregation. Rather, it is a matter of choosing the path that is best for your circumstances. Any investment comes at an opportunity cost: the money can only be spent once and, in choosing to go down one route, other options about the physical layout and use of your buildings are inevitably foreclosed.

Given that there are so many possibilities, we can do little more than skim over the issues involved in each type of project. We might presumptuously compare this to the Ten Commandments: everyone benefits from general guidance about not taking the name of the Lord in vain, and refraining from lying and covetousness, and so on, but only we can discern what that means in the encounters we have from day to day.

Glazed porches

Entrances are meant to facilitate entry – and to do so in a smooth, safe and friendly way. Too many churches fail in this fundamental task. The ideal solution for church doors regularly used by the public is an arrangement that maximizes the movement of people while minimizing the movement of air. To this end, glass has long been used for doors or whole porches. Glazed entrances make a church appear more inviting and improve the experience of crossing the threshold for the first time. If designed well, they can also fit the surrounding stone or brick snugly, improving thermal efficiency. Where appropriate, it is also possible to preserve original features, such as earlier wooden doors.

The standard model for introducing a glazed entrance into a historic building is to create a new porch just inside the original door. This minimizes heat loss while maximizing welcome, because it allows the newcomer to view the space into which they are entering before making the final steps of commitment. The arrangement at St Thomas's, Salisbury, is particularly commendable. Here a glazed porch has been introduced inside the main west portal. St Thomas's is in the city centre, yet just off the main thoroughfare and marketplace. The glazed porch counters the potential for the church to be passed by because it permits pedestrians to glance inside, to slow down, and to consider walking in. This entrance has also been designed with other factors in mind. St Thomas's is a church that hosts many concerts, sometimes for up to 300 people. Within the porch, glass doors open on all three sides (north, south and east) to facilitate maximum ingress and egress at the start and end of events or in an emergency (see overleaf). In addition, the side doors work on an external electronic movement sensor, so as to welcome people in (crucially including those in wheelchairs), combined with a touch button for exit. So, the doors don't keep opening and shutting from movement inside, which reduces draughts and noise irritation.

The porch of St Thomas's, Salisbury.

Churches that have introduced glazed entrances often add imagery or text to the door. Such additions should not reduce the visibility of what lies beyond and thus impair the experience of seamless transition. However, appropriate markings can provide a gentle reminder of a physical barrier and so reduce the risk of injury to flying birds and running children. Etching on the glass offers the smartest solution for this, although removable transfers are cheaper and less permanent if you are uncertain about a design. The most mundane solution is to run translucent strips or dots at the eye-height of children and adults. More creatively, there might be an opportunity to express the church's values through words or a logo. St Mary's, Swansea, has adapted the words of the spiritual encounter between Jacob and God on their glass porch: 'This is none other than the house of God and gate of heaven' (see Gen. 28.17).

One downside of glazed porches is that they can impair internal sightlines, especially if your church has a small footprint. This is not so with St Thomas's nor St Mary's, where the porch is at the west end, well behind all the chairs. Nor is it the case in St Michael's, Mere, a stunning church in a small town in west Wiltshire. Here, a glazed porch leads into a wide north aisle used for social functions, not seating. This would be an issue were such a porch to be installed in my former church of St Michael's, St Albans, because the entrance door leads directly into the main body of the church; an internal porch would obscure views from the southwest pews of the nave. Given these complexities, a glazed entrance was never high up the shopping list when I was the vicar of that church.

An alternative to an internal glazed porch is to be found at St John the Baptist, Tisbury. Here, the parishioners have bisected an unusually long north porch with glass doors, halfway along. This has the benefit of preserving the internal space of the church itself. However, the overall experience is slightly less friendly than the internal porch at Mere because, having passed the glass doors in Tisbury, the visitor still has to continue further down the tunnel of the porch and open the wooden doors beyond.

Toilets

Medieval churches were built long before the advent of flushing loos. People who came to do their business with God left their other business elsewhere. Churches that have been constructed in more recent decades take both matters into account. The provision of toilets and associated amenities make churches much more flexible for worshippers, visitors and other users, and so many older churches have sought innovative ways of retrofitting loos onto their site. Several options and issues should be borne in mind if you are considering such an adaptation.

Some congregations choose to provide toilets in a separate building outside the church itself. This might be within pre-existing structures, such as the Parish Centre at St Michael's, St Albans. Or it might involve a new build, as at St James', Longburton. External toilets might be the way to go if you have a worship space that is small or hard to adapt. Churches that need to introduce water onto the site in order to install a toilet may find it easier to do so within a new build. That said, there are several disadvantages of external loos. Most obviously, anyone wishing to use them will need to leave the main building and walk to the toilet block – less than ideal on a cold, wet winter evening. Any outside loo may therefore also have implications for your churchyard pathways and external lighting. In addition, free-standing new builds are likely to require more materials than internal adaptations and so prove expensive. There may also be tax (VAT) implications to your disadvantage. The planning of any project should take careful account of the terms and conditions of the Listed Places of Worship Grant Scheme in operation at the time.[1]

Given the downsides of an external loo, internal solutions are often preferable. Large barn-like Victorian churches make good candidates for such adaptations because they tend to have spare space and the necessary services on site. That said, toilets still need to be discreet. Ideally, they should be placed where a user can access them without drawing attention to themselves or disturbing others, especially during worship. Locations towards the back of the church are better than at the front. Sensory side effects should also be minimized. Flushes and drainage on wash-hand basins need to be quiet, and an effective but silent extractor is a must unless your church uses a lot of incense. A lobby with more than one door between the congregation and the loo adds to comfort and discretion; this two-door arrangement may be essential in some contexts on hygiene grounds.

A very effective internal loo adaptation may be seen at St Michael's, Mere. It is listed as Grade I by Historic England and is also in the rarer category of being awarded three stars by Simon Jenkins in his famous *England's thousand best churches* (Jenkins, pp. 733–4). The most interesting heritage features of the church are at the east end in the form of a medieval screen, chancel and side chapels. Complementing this, and with a careful eye to architectural context, design and finishings, two toilets have been neatly tucked away under the tower at the west end. They are effectively separated from the body of the nave by an additional set of doors, which leads into an aisle running to the west door.

A third option is a side extension to the church. Several examples of varying success spring to mind.

- A poor example from the 1930s may be seen at St Michael's, St Albans. Here an extension was built onto the northeast corner of the church through a pre-existing external doorway. The primary purpose of the extension was to provide a clergy vestry and, in this regard, the project proved a commodious success. The secondary purpose, the addition of a toilet as an extension off the vestry itself was a disastrous afterthought. Either the loo was intended for the sole use of the vicar (highly exclusive) or for wider congregational purposes, but was only accessible internally via the chancel (highly intrusive). *Nul points.*

- Rather better is the extension built in the 1990s at Clyne Chapel in west Swansea. This church would have been too small for an internal adaptation but a corridor has been inserted into the back corner, leading to a series of small rooms, including a vestry and loo. The location is discreet, both in terms of the internal layout and how the extension sits within the churchyard. My only doubt about this project concerns scale: the additional space created by the extension is relatively small and therefore perhaps limited in its usefulness. Consideration of estimated construction cost per square foot is a helpful guide when comparing the payback value of potential projects.
- Finally, and on a rather different scale, Salisbury Cathedral infilled a dead space between its south transept and chapter house in 2013: effectively the first extension to the cathedral since the Middle Ages. Appropriately titled 'Little Paradise', this facility provides essential storage for furniture, shop stock, IT equipment and flower arranging, as well as a decent number of loos for the continuous flow of people who visit the cathedral throughout the day. *Douze points.*

When planning your toilets, try to include a baby-changing facility if at all possible. This will be important on the grounds of inclusion and will make your building more useful for families with young children. Space could be tight, but a pull-down changing table can be neatly secured to a wall and the cost will be small compared to the overall budget. Forethought may be needed about the sticky issue of nappies as you plan for the hygiene and cleaning of your new facility.

Access is also an important consideration when it comes to toilets. Any new installation (external, internal or extension) will need to comply with the Equalities Act (2010). If you are looking to install a single toilet, it must have space and adaptations appropriate for wheelchair users. The toilet project at St Mary's, Childwick Green, discussed in Chapter 7 is an example of just such a single facility; it is neatly slotted into a complex space between the church and its hall but is nonetheless compliant with the EA.

If you have space for more than one toilet, it is permitted for the second and third toilets to be standard facilities and not necessarily adapted for wheelchairs. I suspect that this balance was in mind at Holy Trinity, Bradford-on-Avon. Here, a standard toilet has been installed under the staircase in the west tower. However, the tower space is too cramped for an accessible toilet. This need has been resolved with an adjacent single-storey extension off the base of the tower.

Standard accessible toilets meet the needs of most disabled people – but not all. Those who have profound and multiple disabilities will require personal assistance to use the toilet or to change incontinence pads. These additional needs can be met through a Changing Places toilet (CPT). CPTs include, for example, a mechanical hoist and a changing bench. Information about the specifications required for such an installation is provided by the Changing Places campaign.[2] A CPT will not be possible or appropriate in many churches. However, when installed, these facilities afford confidence and decency to the quarter of a million people in the UK who need a CPT. A CPT has been brilliantly retrofitted into a barrel-vaulted part of the crypt at Bath Abbey as part of their Footprint Project.[3]

Kitchens

Man shall not live by bread alone. But man cannot live without any bread at all. The offer of hospitality is an important aspect of many world faiths and has been fostered for centuries within Christianity by the monastic tradition. In more recent years, hospitality has been found to play an invaluable part within churches' welcome and evangelistic courses, notably Alpha. So, if you are considering the missional effectiveness of your church, you probably want to review where and how you can offer refreshments.

As with the toilets considered above, the provision of kitchen spaces and equipment within churches varies enormously, depending on the needs of the community (what, who, when), the nature of the building (space available, services installed, heritage constraints), not to mention the funds available. Nonetheless, if you get the ingredients of your kitchen correct, it is likely that you will be able to meet more people in more ways.

Entry-level catering provision comes in the form of a tea point. This would be an immediate blessing to the congregation after a service and, potentially, to other users around the week. Typically, the provision would include a sink, with water and drainage, plus the equipment needed to serve hot drinks: kettles or an urn, cups, cutlery and storage for materials such as coffee and sugar. A little bit more space and a fridge might extend the scope for storing fresh milk and cold drinks – including wine and beer, assuming your congregation is OK with that.

Matters are never simple and, when we start to think around the issue of refreshments, a number of questions spring to mind.

- How protected do you wish your facilities to be? Will they be in a locked room or is a secure cupboard sufficient? Conversely, would you be comfortable with users of your church accessing refreshments for themselves, for example if they are weekday visitors or hirers of your hall? This gesture would be welcoming but would probably create additional mess and cleaning, even if just water is on offer.
- Cleanliness is close to godliness: catering requires hygiene. Surfaces need to be wiped, products have to be within date, and foodstuffs need to be stored where they won't attract flies and rodents. Are you content with serving things such as biscuits on a shared plate (cheaper and friendlier) or do they have to be individually wrapped (more expensive and less environmentally friendly, but less likely to be pre-loved by children rifling in search of their favourites)?
- As your catering provision becomes more complex, more equipment is needed (e.g. different knives and chopping boards), and training and certification will become necessary. Naturally, there is a close relationship between hygiene and health and safety. Is there an appropriately stocked first-aid kit nearby?
- What is the immediate space in which you are serving hospitality? If in church, are you content for worshippers to eat and drink in the main worship space? Do you need to provide separate chairs and tables near your tea point, especially for the less physically mobile?
- Storage is a perennial issue (see Chapter 7, p. 145). Even if you have some cupboards, junk will mount up. But however much storage you have it is never enough, especially if you permit third parties to store materials and equipment on site. Woe betide anyone in the Mothers' Union who touches the cups and saucers of the Women's Institute!

- Catering, even on a small scale, comes with environmental considerations. Single-use plastic receptables should be avoided. Will you choose, instead, washable ceramic mugs (cheaper but laborious) or disposable paper ones (quicker but more expensive and still not very environmentally friendly)? If you are generating food waste, can this be composted in your churchyard? Or can the coffee grounds be given away to keen gardeners?

There are many attractive examples of catering installations in churches. Among the simplest are the cupboards in St Michael's, Mere. These are well situated within an open area at the west end of the north aisle, separated from the main worship space, with room for circulation, and nearby information to browse. St Thomas's, Salisbury, has a similar arrangement behind its organ, albeit in a more confined space, but helpers are able to process many drinks quickly. Holy Trinity, Stourpaine, has a servery that attractively reuses timber from redundant pews. Next up in scale is the walk-in servery room attractively installed in the northwest corner of Holy Trinity, Bradford-on-Avon; it includes a fridge, a dishwasher and cooking facilities, as well as cupboards and a serving hatch.

The kitchen at Holy Trinity, Bradford-on-Avon.

Larger facilities still are more likely to be found in church halls that have weekday uses, which might include commercial functions such as parties. But these facilities can also be very handy for congregations, especially where the hall is contiguous with the church. These can range from domestic kitchens to those with professional stainless steel catering units, such as those at St Mary's, Marshalswick.

The kitchen at St Mary's, Marshalswick.

Cafés

A number of churches have chosen to move beyond the sort of catering facilities that can boost social interaction after services and concerts; instead they have stepped into the territory of cafés. These can operate around the week, provide meeting space for the community, increase footfall through the church building, and generate an additional stream of income for mission. If your leadership team is wondering whether a café might be a good development for your church, there are a few factors to consider.

First, what physical space is available? How much room can you afford to give over? Do you have the necessary services, especially electricity and water? Some churches are fortunate to have underused rooms that can be converted. For many years, St Mary the Virgin in Oxford had a café in the Old Congregation House: a room attached to the northeast corner of the church, with an attractive outside area that opened onto the iconic Radcliffe Square. Although the subject of recent controversy, this café offered a discrete location for food and drink that was physically integral to the church but that could be accessed from outside if an event or service were taking place in the nave.

Other churches have cafés situated within the main worship space itself. The café at the west end of the southern aisle in St Mary's, Swansea, is unobtrusive; it is tucked behind pillars, within a large space. By contrast, the cafés in St Mary Aldermary in the City of London[4] and All Saints, Hereford, are wholly integrated within the traditional worship area. These examples pose questions about the extent to which a church sees the café and worship space as complementary or distinct from each other. Is the configuration and furnishing of a café such that chairs can be turned around and integrated into an act of worship? Or – spinning the question on its head – are you seeking to create a 'café church', in which worship and teaching can be delivered to groups seated around tables within the less formal layout of comfy chairs?

Second, what is your commercial model? Some cafés are run in part or whole by volunteers. This model depends on the availability of people who are willing to give time as part of their Christian vocation or service to the wider community. That café in St Mary's, Swansea, has been supported for many years on a bedrock of people from the congregations. However, as a café grows, paid leadership may be needed to ensure efficiency of service and safe, hygienic systems. The pressures and demands of busier cafés are likely to require a solely paid workforce.

If you have salaried staff in your café, what financial framework will you choose? Should you retain control and employ in-house staff? This is likely to accrue more surplus; but it will also create greater hassle in terms of human resource management: hiring, firing, training and payroll. The alternative is to grant the café as a franchise to a professional company. This should protect the church from day-to-day administrative worries and may make for a more predictable income; but it could lead to challenges regarding the use of a shared space. What agreement would you have in place with your catering contractor for when a funeral or one-off event happens in the church?

Tying together the issues of physical space and financial model is an underlying question about motivation. Why do you want a café? If you wish to generate a solid stream of funding for the ministry of your church and there is demand from people nearby, then a high-end franchise might be the way to go. If, on the other hand, you wish a café to be more actively involved in your mission to your local community, especially if you are seeking to reach out to the more vulnerable, then you may be better served by simpler facilities. These can be staffed by the congregation and capable of being used as a relaxed venue for alternative worship.

Office space

The amenities above will directly benefit members of the public who use your church. We all need toilets and catering. We don't all need office space – but many churches do. Provision of facilities for desktop working can assist the mission of your church in two ways. It can enable behind-the-scenes functions that facilitate up-front human interaction. And it could become a source of income if you have enough space to hire (some of) it out to others.

At the most basic level, office space means a desk and chair. This was the sort of arrangement I had when a curate at St Mary's in Swansea. St Mary's is a vast building, with side rooms that could be commandeered for new purposes. To the north of the nave was a secluded and unused chapel. It had its own door and so could be separately heated. There was enough room for a desk and a few chairs to provide a simple space for the rector to meet people in privacy, and to undertake desk work while on site. A similar arrangement was created for me, the curate, on the other side of the building, in the base of the tower. Effectively a converted storeroom, my tower office was not appropriate for pastoral conversations; it had the added blessing of cannabis smoke drifting under the external door from youths outside. Albeit cheap, these arrangements met our needs and enabled the clergy to be available in church on weekdays. If we wanted to concentrate on reading and writing, this was best done at home. But if we had simple desk-based tasks to process, it was possible inside St Mary's, where we were likely to have many ad hoc conversations with those passing through.

Most church offices are more deliberate and permanent than those at St Mary's, Swansea. Some will be used by clergy; others by professional administrators or unpaid helpers. Ideally, these have been purpose-built, either at the same time as the church or as an extension to an older building. A purpose-built office should enable the right amount of space for the needs of the church, an efficient layout, and the relevant services, such as IT cabling. That said, needs are rapidly changing as computers have become smaller and communication has taken an increasingly digital and wireless format. Less space is required for apparatus such as printers, and churches may need less storage for paper and other gear. New equipment brings new requirements, of course, and churches, like other organizations, have responsibilities for providing desk-based colleagues (paid or unpaid) with facilities that conform to health and safety standards, such as display screen equipment (DSE) at the right height and angle.[5]

Some churches may find more commercial opportunities to capitalize on the need for office facilities. If your church has significant internal air space that is surplus to requirements, is there scope to create an office that could be used by third-party partners? An early example of this was inserted into St Barnabas, Uplands, a suburb of Swansea, in the 1990s. It was discerned that St Barnabas was too large for the needs of its congregation, at a time when the diocese of Swansea and Brecon was seeking to rationalize its southern administrative hub from a separate building on the outskirts of the city. To bring these two requirements together, the west end of St Barnabas was given over to a new administration centre, which included office space, a print room, kitchen and loos. Central to this scheme was also the need for a meeting room where the bishop could hold small gatherings when in the southern half of the diocese. Larger meetings could spill out into the church, and a mezzanine gallery was created above the office, so there is still plenty of seating for larger services when required. A more radical and dramatic example of the same principle can be seen in St Jude's, Kensington; here, a Victorian church has been repurposed as the London home of St Mellitus theological college (2009–12). This amazing conversion has retained a central worship space, while using glass screens to turn the aisles and galleries into meeting space, offices and a library; the crypt houses lecture and teaching rooms.[6]

These examples from Swansea and London both involve partnerships between a local church and another ecclesiastical organization. There is doubtless a synergy of mutual understanding in this. In other contexts, however, I wonder whether third-party commercial arrangements might be possible, with a worship area retained but a large air space reduced and put to greater use during the working week? This need not require a permanent lease: there has been a growth of demand for flexible hot desking that can be hired on a temporary basis. If decent wifi and refreshments are available, could your church offer a convivial base for weekday hot desking? Alternatively, as my former colleague Charles King observes, 'If a fully spec'd-up office space is not an option, how about a simpler space for a homework club or similar? Blend with basic hospitality (refreshments, bean bags, etc.), and it begins to push the missional buttons for growing younger [congregations] …'

Shops

Jesus didn't approve of profiteering from religion (Matt. 10.5–10), nor of worshipping the god of money (Matt. 6.24), nor of misappropriating holy places for retail functions (Mark 11.15–17). Nonetheless, churches need to break even if they are to continue their mission and ministry. Jesus' teaching is about priorities: Christians do not serve Mammon – but might Mammon be put to work in service of Jesus? If your congregation is open to commercial activity within your building, you may wish to think about a shop.

Some of the principles considered above about cafés are equally applicable to shops. Where would you place one? How comfortable are you with commercial intrusion into your worship space? How might the shop be staffed?

Most important, however, is the question about for whom it is intended. The answer to this will give rise to two types of shop.

Traditionally, larger churches have tended to sell religious artefacts (Bibles and prayer books, icons and music), alongside merchandise about the church itself (guidebooks and trinkets), and maybe 'heritage' products from the local area (chutney, soap, and so on). These items might appeal to rather different customers: worshippers looking to resource their life with God; visitors wishing for a memento of the church; and the general public seeking small gifts for special occasions. Churches with shops like this should reflect on the balance they are seeking to strike between these rather different markets and recent trends, such as the decline of small independent bookshops, including high street Christian retailers. Help is at hand in the form of the Cathedral and Church Shops Association, a not-for-profit, non-denominational group that seeks to support the work of the Church through retailing.[7]

A few churches have branched out from this model and established secular retail partnerships with community shops. Often these are in areas where valued services, such as the post office and local stores, have become unviable, but where a partnership between a church building and a need for basic goods and services has proven mutually beneficial. This in turn provides a blessing for the wider community: reducing isolation and loneliness and enabling residents to stay in their homes rather than being forced to move to bigger settlements.

If this is something that you might be considering for your church, a good place to start is the Plunkett Foundation, an organization committed to fostering community-owned businesses around the UK.[8] Plunkett knows that when community shops are located in places of worship, they can also help to keep historic buildings open by generating income through rent, attracting more people through the door, and increasing opportunities to apply for funding. The Plunkett website has inspiring stories of churches where a partnership shop has been installed, it also hosts a report, sponsored by the Benefact Trust, about unlocking the potential of places of worship for community businesses.

A great example of this sort of partnership can be found in a remote, rural corner of Wiltshire at the Chalke Valley Stores.[9] Here, a small chapel of the United Reformed Church has been converted into a buzzy seven-day-a-week community hub. The chapel is ideally located, adjacent to the main road through the village. A small parking area has been shaped at the front, with bays for half a dozen vehicles. From this, a ramp and steps lead up to the main door in the gable end of the chapel, where a shop, with a decent range of goods, has been inserted. I was astonished at how many products were available, including fresh fruit, vegetables, meat and dairy. There is even a post office squeezed into one corner.

But there is more. Pass through the shop, which is in the back 40 per cent of the chapel, and an internal door opens onto the front 60 per cent. Here a mixture of sofas and comfortable chapel chairs are attractively arranged around tables, where customers can sit and enjoy refreshments from a servery. Not an inch of space has been lost, with toilets added at the far end and extra storage created on a mezzanine above the shop.

When I visited the Chalke Valley Stores on an ordinary weekday in the school holidays, several dozen people came through in the time it took me to consume some coffee and cake. There was a relaxed feeling throughout. A farmer and his son hopped off their tractor for a drink. Several grannies were nattering over quiche. A string of customers was using the shop and post office.

But Mammon has not taken over: this is still a valued place of worship. The chairs in the café can be rearranged for services of up to thirty people, centred on a simple wooden cross hung in the apse. A noticeboard outside advertises the times of services to the stream of customers passing through the shop and café.

The need for partnerships with services such as the post office may seem most obvious in rural areas. However, examples can flourish in bustling cities too.[10]

Community partnerships

The principle of sharing a church with a third-party partner for greater mutual impact is by no means confined to offices and shops. Almost anything is possible if there is synergy of purpose and need. A few more examples will suffice.

Shortly after the diocese of Swansea and Brecon built its office hub in St Barnabas, Uplands (see p. 82 above), it developed two further projects to share church buildings. Both of these involved an external partner, both brought considerable community benefit, and both secured the long-term future of a place of worship.

St John, Hafod, and St Matthew's, High Street, were churches beset with a familiar collection of co-morbidities. St Matthew's is situated in the twilight zone of the city centre, where small shops have collapsed and substance misuse and homelessness are rife. For its part, Hafod has experienced rapid social change through the migration of new communities into the city. By the 1990s, the traditional bases of both congregations had eroded and giving levels were low. Both buildings were unfit for purpose and both were beyond a point where they could be rescued by the Church alone.

The solution for St John's, Hafod, lay in affordable housing. A lease was signed with Gwalia, a housing association, to build a series of flats.

The nave was converted and an extension built out of the west end of the church. Part of the deal created enough funds for the historic chancel to be refurbished as a smaller, warmer and more comfortable place of worship. Without this intervention, the church would surely have closed and been demolished or redeveloped. Through this partnership (now a quarter of a century later), a base remains for a faithful congregation, as well as attractive housing in a historic building. (see p. 40 for a more recent, similar example in Radlett, Hertfordshire.)

St Matthew's, Swansea, presented an even more forbidding prospect. A solution was found by turning the challenge of its location, in an area of multiple deprivation, into an opportunity for service among the most vulnerable and needy in the city. The diocese entered a lease arrangement with a charity called the Cyrenians. Named after Simon of Cyrene, who helped to bear Jesus' cross (Mark 15.21), this organization ran support programmes and facilities for those on the streets of the city. Through the lease, the Cyrenians refitted the rear of St Matthew's to a very high standard in order to provide healthy food, showers, a laundry, basic medical facilities, and a safe place where the homeless and those in need could meet with charitable and statutory social care providers. Meanwhile, and similar to St John, Hafod, the east end of the church was refreshed as a flexible, warm worship space, retaining the traditional stained glass and other heritage features of the building.

There's been a lot of change in St Matthew's since I knew it. It no longer has an Anglican congregation and the Cyrenians have relinquished their lease. However, the principles of the conversion project live on. A group called The Hill Church[11] has taken over the site, offering worship in the tradition of the Newfrontiers movement. The Hill Church have created a separate charity, Matthew's House,[12] to operate social action work through the rear of the property.

Other options?!

There are further possibilities for sharing church buildings. This can be done either through a long-term lease, as with the Swansea examples, or through short-term letting. When I was Warden of Church Hostel in Bangor (2007–12), a number of groups used our chapel for exercise activities. The chapel had a warm carpet, and we used folding chairs that could be easily cleared away. The chapel was even hired by the local authority, once a year, as a polling station. 'Might it be an issue for some voters to cast their ballots in a place of worship?' I asked the council officer who came to inspect the property. He thought not. If he didn't mind people placing their crosses beneath the rather larger one hanging from the ceiling, I certainly didn't. The imagery, community integration, footfall and extra income all worked from my perspective.

I have been approached a couple of times during my ministry by other Christian denominations wanting to lead worship, according to their own traditions, in the church where I worked. More prayer is surely a good thing and, in the interests of ecumenical relations, I would always seek to respond constructively to such enquiries. A couple of times this has proved very fruitful. The church where I served as a curate was used regularly by a multilingual Eastern Orthodox congregation and occasionally by the German Lutheran Church. The Lutherans also made use of my parish church in St Albans for their annual celebration of St Martin's Day.

That said, not all ecumenical approaches can be successfully converted into partnerships. The needs of the new congregation may not readily mesh with those of the host – especially as both are likely to want to use the building on Sundays. During my time as a vicar in St Albans, I was approached by a congregation from the Oriental Orthodox tradition about establishing a weekly service in the daughter church of St Mary's, Childwick Green. Exciting though the possibility was, their congregation was probably too large for our building, our furniture would have frustrated some of their liturgical movement (e.g. prostration), and they would have needed on-site storage for liturgical items, such as icons, which was beyond what we would have been able to provide. Advice from the archdeacon was a big help as we sought a gentle way of saying no.

With fewer people living in the countryside, it may seem that there are not so many options for partnerships in rural churches as in urban areas. However, one opportunity catching the imagination of some village churches is 'champing'. Think camping meets churches. The Churches Conservation Trust (CCT) markets champing as 'sleepovers with soul' and has established a website to bring together all the churches that are offering this opportunity. Although the CCT was founded to care for redundant churches, churches that are formally still open and used for regular worship are welcome to join the champing network. There is a handy form on the CCT website for churches that want to find out more.[13] Hirers who book a church through the champing website have exclusive hire of the building, can take dogs as well as people, and can rest secure in the knowledge that their stay is helping to support the maintenance of historic buildings for years to come.

Projects that make a difference

Of the seven chapters in this book, this one has been the hardest to write. I wonder if this is because it covers such a diverse range of possible projects and partnerships. The options are open-ended but blue-sky thinking has to be balanced by the bounds of realism. Moreover, while we have been considering projects that have many similarities, the delivery of each in the context of an individual church requires bespoke plans and execution. Given this open-endedness, I wonder if it has also been the hardest to write because it poses some of the biggest questions about the ambition for, and vocation and future of, each of our church buildings.

Notes

1 https://listed-places-of-worship-grant.dcms.gov.uk (accessed 12.3.25).
2 https://www.changing-places.org (accessed 12.3.25).
3 https://www.astorbannerman.co.uk/news/historic-bath-abbey-gets-new-changing-places-toilet/; bathabbey.org/footprint (accessed 12.3.25).
4 https://www.thecityofldn.com/directory/host-cafe (accessed 12.3.25).
5 https://www.hse.gov.uk/pubns/ck1.htm (accessed 12.3.25).
6 https://en.wikipedia.org/wiki/St_Jude%27s_Church,_Kensington (accessed 12.3.25); https://www.zehnder.co.uk/en/sectors-knowledge/zehnder-academy/case-studies/st-judes-church (accessed 12.3.25).
7 https://www.cathedralandchurchshops.com/index.php (accessed 12.3.25).
8 https://www.plunkett.co.uk (accessed 12.3.25).
9 https://chalkevalleystores.co.uk (accessed 12.3.25).
10 https://thesherriffcentre.co.uk (accessed 12.3.25).
11 https://the-hill.co (accessed 12.3.25).
12 https://matthewshouse.org.uk (accessed 12.3.25).
13 https://www.champing.co.uk (accessed 12.3.25).

5

Carbon reduction

Climate change and Christian mission

Climate change is the greatest challenge facing humanity. It threatens the very future of life on earth. We know the problem: scientists have been warning for decades that our planet is, on average, warming year-on-year. This is already having devastating consequences for communities and eco-systems around the world. Increasingly extreme weather conditions are creating storms and flooding in some places, and drought and wildfires in others. Rising sea levels owing to melting ice caps are threatening the viability of low-lying settlements. And, as so often, it is the poorest and most vulnerable who are hit the hardest: climate change is forcing migration away from parts of the developing world and is pushing some species of plants and animals to the brink of extinction.

In knowing the problem, we also know the cause: the atmosphere of our planet is changing because of emissions associated with industrialization. A process that began in eighteenth-century Britain spread across Europe in the nineteenth century and throughout the world by the final quarter of the twentieth century. Most economies have shifted from a predominantly agricultural base to a modern urban society. Key to this transition has been the burning of fossil fuels such as coal, oil and gas. Combustion of these fuels releases carbon dioxide which, along with other gases emitted though industrial processes and domestic devices, has a propensity to trap energy from the sun and so heat up the planet.

In knowing the cause of the problem, we also know the solution: new technology is available and changes are possible in how we live our lives, which together will reduce our reliance on processes and products that adversely affect the climate. The governments of the world agreed at the United Nations Climate Change Conference in Paris in 2015 (sometimes known as COP 21) to reduce emissions in such a way as to try to restrict the global temperature rise in the twenty-first century to 1.5°C above pre-industrial levels.

However, even though we know the solution, we also know how unrealistic that Paris goal of 1.5°C appears. The complexity of the challenge is because everyone is implicated: the lifestyles that we take for granted revolve around what we consume, our domestic comforts, travel choices, and so on. It can be done: when I was growing up, dire warnings were issued by scientists about a hole in the ozone layer. This had been caused by the release of CFC gases from aerosols and other products. It took international agreement and a collective effort to replace CFCs with alternatives that were less damaging to the planet. The emissions curve was reversed and the ozone layer is recovering. However, the challenge of decreasing climate-warming gases is much greater than tackling CFCs. This is because it's not just a matter of changing our deodorant and fridges; it's about our whole way of life. It will also require action across all elements of society: individuals, organizations and governments. It's not going to be cheap and everyone has a part to play if we are going to succeed. Governments can take a lead, reach agreement with other countries, and set the legislative framework. Individuals must make behavioural changes at home. And institutions need to revolutionize how we construct, heat, light and operate our shared spaces, such as offices, factories, hospitals, schools – and places of worship.

Christians approach the challenge of climate change not just as an existential threat to humanity. We also view the issue through the lens of theology: our attitude to carbon reduction is informed by what we believe about the world as God's creation, about the sinful tendency of people to do things for short-term or selfish gain, and about the values with which the gospel compels us to conduct our lives in the interests of others. A considerable amount of thinking, praying and writing has been done in the field of environmental theology in recent decades. This has shifted most Christians' outlook away from an approach that sought to justify human supremacy over nature (for example, as read from God's gift of dominion in Gen. 1.26) and towards a better appreciation of our duty to collaborate for the long-term survival of the planet.

Many churches and Christian leaders have issued statements about climate change. Pope Francis and Patriarch Bartholomew as leaders of the two largest Christian denominations have been outspoken, for example in the papal encyclical *Laudato si'*.[1] *The Bishop's Letter About the Climate* (second edition 2020) from the Lutheran Church of Sweden is another example of a widely respected prophetic voice on this issue.[2] Much has been said about the role that humans might play as 'stewards' of the world, caring for God's creation of which we ourselves are a part (Northcott; White; Bauckham; Holtham).

A few Christians are in denial about climate change. A few more are waiting for God to provide a miraculous solution. And there are even a few who think that global warming is God's way of hastening the end times. While I do not deny the theoretical possibility of direct divine intervention in the global ecosystem, it would seem much more pragmatic for humans to accept responsibility for the damage we have done to God's incredible planet, and to acknowledge that the power is in our hands to make a difference. God's providence will work itself out through the steps that we take to lower our carbon consumption.

For Anglicans, the Christian duty of environmental responsibility is articulated as part of the 'Five Marks of Mission', which are recognized by the global Anglican Communion as characteristic of the life and work of the Church.[3] The fifth Mark of Mission asks us 'to strive to safeguard the integrity of creation, and sustain and renew the life of the earth'. However, environmental responsibility is also implicit in the other Marks because we know that climate change is a source of social injustice, due to its disproportionate impact on the poorest communities (the fourth Mark), which in turn creates practical human needs. And we are called to respond in love to these (the third Mark).

Climate change also has big implications for the foci of this book. Together we are reflecting on how our buildings can be made fit for purpose in the twenty-first century. We need places of worship and gathering that meet modern expectations if we are going to be effective in evangelism (the first Mark) and discipleship (the second Mark). We can't do without heat and light. Like the rest of society, Christians are implicated and enmeshed. Given this, churches have a vital role to play, not only in making our contribution to bear down on global emissions of carbon dioxide, but also to show how this promotes God's vision of a fairer society. As we are seeing throughout this book, there is a direct line of influence between our values and the ways in which we maintain and run our churches, halls and other facilities. By their very nature, kingdom buildings must integrate theory and practice if they are to be effective beacons of the gospel.

This is easier said than done. The many challenges with which we have been grappling in this book are writ large when it comes to carbon reduction. Lots of churches were built centuries before modern heating and lighting. Their heritage is often listed and they are often hard to adapt to make more efficient. And this is an issue not just for our places of worship but also for the halls, housing and schools controlled by the Church. The limitations of people, finance and systems that we have considered in other chapters can also become factors for fear and inertia when it comes to carbon reduction. However, by the same token, the positive principles that run throughout this book are also applicable to meeting the challenge of climate change: know your context and form a plan; start small but strive for the long term; integrate these projects into your wider strategy.

The problem of carbon consumption runs across so much of what we do as a society, so the solutions must be equally comprehensive. Green thinking has gone from being a fringe pursuit, a generation ago, to a watchword that is built into all projects and systems. The challenge of carbon reduction is massive, but we must never look on it as too big to tackle. And if churches cannot take a lead on this, we will have no moral authority with which to speak into the other great issues of our day.

Where to start?

The General Synod of the Church of England voted in 2020 that the whole of the Church should be net zero carbon within a decade. Words are easy, action is harder – not least in the Church of England, because the General Synod has few levers with which it can compel the constituent parts of the Church (dioceses, parishes, cathedrals, schools and theological education institutions) to make the necessary changes to our habits and systems. Into this gap, the Church has inserted a guide to the issues and options: *The Church of England routemap to net zero carbon by 2030*.[4] The *Routemap* is a framework that can inform and encourage. In addition, the Church Commissioners have earmarked a fund of £200 million to be released in three tranches to assist the constituent parts of the Church towards carbon neutrality.

The goal of making the Church of England carbon neutral by 2030 has been widely ridiculed. Julian Allwood, Professor of Engineering and the Environment at the University of Cambridge, demonstrated at the National Cathedrals Conference in Newcastle in 2022 that a date of 2050 was ambitious but achievable, assuming that churches implemented a programme of reducing their carbon footprint by an average of 6 per cent a year.

It is important not to beat ourselves up about arbitrary targets. Conversely, this must not become an excuse for doing nothing; we need to be straining every sinew to go as far as we can as quickly as we can.

It is also clear that the Church Commissioners' fund of £200 million, substantial though it is, will not touch the sides of what is needed for every diocese, parish, cathedral and church school to reach the goal of carbon neutrality. What this money can do is to act as seedcorn funding to get a few projects up and running to inspire other churches to start along the path they need to travel. To this end, the first tranche of the Commissioners' funds will encourage churches with easy wins and demonstration projects that other churches can hopefully emulate.

Measuring the footprint

As we have seen with other practical projects, the first thing that local churches need to do is understand their context and buildings. We need to know our carbon footprint and what is causing it if we are to plan to reduce it. To assist this process, the Church of England has produced an 'Energy Footprint Tool'. This is an online platform into which a church can submit its utility meter readings and which then calculates the carbon consumption of that church. There is another website with the confusingly similar name of 'Energy Toolkit' for measuring carbon consumption by dioceses, cathedrals and church schools. Other denominations may have equivalent devices. If your denomination does not, there are generic online calculators.

The Church of England's Energy Footprint Tool provides collated data about a church's carbon consumption per annum and an energy performance pyramid similar to those you find on fridges and in the atria of public buildings. These offer an at-a-glance assessment of performance on a scale from A to G: good to bad to truly very ugly. The data and diagrams from these devices make for interesting, if alarming, reading. The first thing to look for is a building's gross and net consumption figures. Gross consumption is the total amount of utilities used. Net consumption offsets this against things such as electricity generated on site through solar panels. Ultimately it is this net figure that we are aiming to minimize and eventually eliminate entirely.

Numbers of course are sometimes hard to visualize. One way in which you can make your data more meaningful is to consider how many trees are needed to absorb your annual carbon output. This in itself is a bit of a finger-in-the-air test because an online search will give you many different conversion ratios, presumably because of variations in the type and size of tree. Nonetheless, the working ratio given to me by an architect, whom I trust, is that it takes 40 mature trees to absorb 1 tonne of carbon dioxide every year. So if your house has a net footprint of 10 tonnes of carbon dioxide a year (not unrealistic for many houses), you'll need a garden with 400 mature trees for your house to be carbon neutral (rather less typical). It is sobering stuff. The annual carbon output of most churches will be much higher than that of a typical house.

If this carbon dioxide-to-tree ratio seems rather terrifying, the silver lining of obtaining a baseline assessment of carbon consumption is that it is likely to incentivize change. Moreover, repeating the assessment on an annual basis will allow a community to celebrate the progress it is making towards carbon neutrality – or to sound alarm bells if the numbers start to go in the wrong direction.

Of course, an element of interpretation is always required. For example, Salisbury Cathedral has a vast air space and so our carbon footprint per square metre is atrocious; it gives us a big red 'G' rating, right at the bottom of the energy pyramid. However, we are also blessed with a quarter of a million visitors per year and thousands of others who come to worship, concerts and other events. This means our carbon footprint per person hour is completely at the other end of the scale; our consumption per capita is excellent compared to churches with a lower footfall.

Revolving the problem further, however, the Church of England Energy Footprint Tool and Energy Toolkit only calculate direct energy consumption: i.e. what a building uses in terms of gas and electricity.

They do not calculate indirect carbon consumption, which includes travel to and from church and the carbon needed to make the products used in our buildings. In the case of a church, this might be hymn books, office equipment, food and drink – ultimately even the 'embedded' carbon from the construction of the building itself. I recently saw estimated carbon figures for a school with a very inefficient building. However, its direct heating and lighting use was dwarfed by its indirect carbon consumption through classroom materials, travel for educational purposes, school lunches and so on.

Net zero action plans

In working out the size of your carbon footprint, you will also start to understand the sources of your carbon consumption. With this information at your fingertips, you have what you need to begin to plan for change. It would probably be useful to document your thinking in a net zero action plan that lists your goals, hurdles and next steps. Heating and lighting should be at the forefront of your thinking, but there will probably be other areas where marginal improvements can be made. Data loggers are available to use to get a better breakdown of utility consumption and identify where electricity is being used inefficiently, for example through devices left on overnight.

Before we come to specific opportunities, I would offer a few general observations about planning and implementing changes for carbon reduction. First, there is a plethora of online advice from people who are keen to tell you what to do. As with everything on the Internet, much of it is helpful but not all of it is accurate. Moreover, the sheer scale of this information can seem a little daunting. So choose what you read with caution.

To narrow your options, I heartily commend the online resources of Church Care.[5] Its material is particularly useful, especially the dedicated net zero carbon playlist on its YouTube channel.[6] These videos show experts on carbon reduction speaking about topics such as heat pumps, solar panels and electric cars in a way that those who, like me, are lay people to such issues can understand. While some of the advice on Church Care is specific to the Church of England, much will also be relevant to other denominations. For those who are feeling a little more adventurous – maybe I mean nerdy – I also commend the Technical Tuesday webinars produced by Historic England. These videos take the issues and advice around heritage conservation to a much deeper level.[7] Historic England has also synthesized the need for carbon reduction in tandem with its principles about conservation care within the framework of the English planning system; this is documented in its advice note titled *Adapting historic buildings for energy and carbon efficiency*.[8]

Second, there is a shadow side to the voluminous advice on the Internet: namely, that there is a dearth of practical skills on the ground. I suspect that these two are not disconnected: it is easy to reach a wide audience through talking about the issues online; it is much more laborious to make a practical difference. The good news is that a transition is occurring; new technicians are being trained to work on the heat pumps, solar panels and electric-vehicle (EV) chargers of the future. Young people coming into mechanical and electrical engineering are adding to these skills. However, there are very few retirees from the sector who can lend time to churches – or even to DACs – as they navigate the opportunities and pitfalls of low-carbon technology. Given this, those looking to undertake carbon-reduction projects can expect a long wait on companies' order books and/or high prices. A silver lining might be that churches of size and antiquity will represent 'iconic' projects that might pique the interests of engineers more than less exciting buildings.

Not only is the base of suitably qualified engineers quickly expanding, some of the technology is still rapidly developing. I sense that this is particularly the case with heat pumps, having seen several projects with heat exchangers that weren't working; where the heat pumps failed to integrate with other parts of the heating system; or which emitted inadequate heat for the size of space requiring warmth. In the words of one colleague, low-carbon engineering represents the 'bleeding edge' of technology.

It is by no means all doom and gloom: the technology that works in theory can also be made to work in practice. For example, I have been privileged to look behind the scenes at the National Trust house at Kingston Lacy in Dorset, during and after the installation of a ground-source heat-pump scheme. I was blown away by the results – more than adequate levels of heat were being delivered to the historic rooms of the house, and the output was being carefully monitored to see where further efficiencies could be achieved.

Given the above, I am a realist, not a pessimist: we need to choose our agents with care; we may also need to wait longer or pay more to get the right job done. That said, considering everything that we know about climate change, we cannot bury our heads in the sand – which brings me neatly to my third general observation. In seeking to act on climate change, it is very easy to get distracted. We need realistic plans that maintain momentum over the long term. And we require focused plans that avoid the temptation to greenwash or to be distracted by easy wins that are laudable but ultimately represent a diversion. For instance, there are lots of good things churches can and should be doing with ecology, some examples of which are discussed in the next chapter, but they mustn't become a distraction from the hard graft of bearing down on carbon consumption.

Heating

Moving from generalities to specifics, we need to start with heating. This is because heating is likely to be the largest contributor to the carbon footprint of your church, especially if your heating is delivered through gas- or oil-fired boilers. Sorting out your heating is likely to be the holy grail of carbon reduction in your context – and therefore also the most complicated, lengthy and expensive.

While you plan for your future heating requirements, two important considerations should be given to your existing system; they may represent low-hanging fruit that can be plucked quickly at relatively low cost. First, is your heating system being run as efficiently as possible? If you have a boiler, speak to your annual service engineer to discuss the implications of reducing the flow temperature, maybe from 75°C to 70°C or from 70°C to 65°C. You might like to review this in tandem with considering the optimum output temperature on your thermostat. Here in Salisbury Cathedral, for example, we know that the system will not achieve a room temperature above 16°C during the winter; we simply should not bother trying to crank it any higher. Another variation of the same game is to consider the length of your heating season. There was a running joke in my previous parish that the vicar considered the heating season to run from December to January, while some of my colleagues thought it should last from September to June. In reality, there are a few weeks to play with in October and April, which can make a marginal difference without frightening people off with the cold. Shaving a fortnight off the beginning and end of the heating season in Salisbury Cathedral has reduced our direct annual emissions by several tonnes of carbon dioxide, one of the biggest single impacts that we can make to our carbon footprint until such time as the heating system is replaced.

The second and rather less low-hanging fruit that you can pluck is around the thermal efficiency of your building: basically, how leaky it is. If you can lengthen the time of your 'air-change cycle', you will retain more hot air within the building. Old churches are notoriously draughty because of the way in which they were built, and the materials used in their construction. Moreover, fewer interventions will be permissible in the heritage context of listed churches. Nonetheless, making your building as efficient as possible is likely to be a necessary preliminary to installing any future low-carbon heating system. Minimizing heat loss within the bounds of what is possible and cost-effective is an important stepping stone towards your goal.

Your in-house church team will probably be able to undertake a preliminary review of thermal efficiency and maybe even make some in-house improvements. Some interventions will be more sensitive or substantial, and advice can be sought from your architect if necessary.

The problem with draughts is that they cause air circulation chambers and temperature differentials. Often it is the perception of this air movement that can make a place seem cold. Thus, by reducing draughts, you do not need to make an appreciable difference to the average temperature of the building before it starts to feel warmer.

Three areas to which you should pay particular attention are windows, roofs and doors. Church windows are often single-glazed and are prone to cracking, smashing and weaknesses around the leadwork. Any obvious holes should be temporarily patched and a maintenance plan developed for more substantive repairs. Church roofs are harder to access of course and cannot be insulated like domestic loft spaces; but are there any actions that can be taken to block holes, for instance under the eaves, either immediately or at a time of future maintenance? Church doors are an obvious source of draughts because they open to the outside world. They can also shrink or warp with age and so develop gaps between door and rebate. I am not a fan of heavy curtains on the inside of church doors because they look dark and imposing; but are there other ways in which draughts can be minimized, especially if a door is not in regular use? With doors that you do use, if you have a welcomer near the entrance during services, can they keep an eye on the door as well as the people who come through, in order to help reduce draughts? Larger buildings may benefit from installing an electric heat curtain above the doorway: the sort of device that keeps supermarket entrances warm in the winter.

In tandem with taking these initial steps, you can also research some future heating options. The first consideration here is to decide whether you want to heat people or air space. If your place of worship is used for just a few hours a week and/or for a congregation that is small relative to the size of the building, and/or in a building with a rapid air-change cycle, then the most efficient solution is probably to heat the people within the building, rather than the building's air space. Assuming you are on the grid and therefore not reduced to issuing blankets as the congregation enters, your most cost-effective solution is likely to lie in direct electrical heating: underpew panels or heated cushions. Given that heat rises, I think that these forms of direct electrical heating are always preferable to the infra-red scalp burning alternatives from overhead panels or chandeliers.

Further reflection might lead you to reexamine your style of worship. For those who are able, a bit more standing and movement can break up long periods of chilly sitting. If these options do not appeal, my mind turns to those churches that have been able to create smaller spaces within their building (e.g. with glass screens) where it is easier to heat space and not just people. A successful example can be found at St John the Baptist, Tisbury, where the chancel has been glazed off. The main worship space remains in the nave, but with the potential to reduce draughts from the chancel in front; a well-sealed chapel has effectively been created to the east of the chancel arch for services of up to about 40 people. Less successful from a missional point of view are those congregations that relocate from their church building for some months of the year. This creates a dislocation between congregation and building; it can also make it harder for newcomers to find their way into the worshipping community. 'Are we in the church or school this week?

Not sure; let's not bother going.' If you find that it really is more comfortable worshipping in the school than the church, has the time come to make the break and move into the school all year round?

Churches that are used for longer periods and by more people are likely to be looking to heat the air space within their building rather than the people who use it. For most churches in this category, especially those beyond urban areas, the future will lie in heat pumps. Crudely speaking, heat pumps are 'reverse fridges'. They extract heat from a source. This is then compressed to raise the temperature of a liquid, which can then deliver heat to the intended destination, be that a home, office, school or church. Through this system, more heat energy is supplied to the target space than is consumed in fuel: a multiplier effect known as the Coefficient of Performance (CoP). Whereas a gas boiler might have a CoP of 0.8 and a direct electric heater of 1.0, heat pumps have a CoP that is much higher. Bear in mind that electricity costs four times as much as gas per unit of energy. This means that any heat pump that can obtain a CoP of 3.2 will be no more expensive to run than a conventional boiler (4 x 0.8).

With a heat-pump system that is powered by electricity, the carbon consumption of your heating will then be determined by the mix of sources through which your electricity is generated. Increasingly, churches are paying for 'green tariff' electricity. For green electricity, a supplier charges the market rate for generating electricity from renewable sources. It has been possible, for a number of years, for parishes of the Church of England and Church in Wales to buy green electricity through the Parish Buying Scheme (PBS).[9] Even for those not on a green tariff, the proportion of electricity generated from fossil fuels is diminishing year by year, as the National Grid moves away from coal and gas. It is pursuing a target of decarbonization by 2035 through supplying a greater mix of wind, nuclear and solar power.[10]

There are three types of heat pump, differentiated by whether they obtain heat from an air, ground or water source.

1 Most common are air source heat pumps (ASHPs); these look like large air-conditioning units and are increasingly seen by the side of buildings or on roofs. An ASHP is the cheapest type of heat pump to install but the most expensive to run: it generates a CoP of 2.0 to 2.5. The challenge of an ASHP is that winter air temperatures mean that

the CoP is at its lowest and least efficient at the very time when the demand for space heating is at its highest.

2 Ground source heat pumps (GSHPs) extract heat from the ground through a long array of pipes. These pipes can be laid horizontally just below the surface of the ground. However, a horizontal array requires a lot of land and so the array is usually drilled vertically or diagonally, often down to depths of 200 metres or more. Once installed, the pipework of a GSHP array might last for up to a century, even though the heat pumps into which those pipes feed will need replacing every 20 years or so, just as you would replace a boiler today. To squash two myths: GSHPs do not damage the water table because the pipes that are run through the ground are entirely sealed. The system is 'closed'. Nor does GSHP heating have anything to do with fracking. Given the complexities of drilling, GSHPs have much higher installation costs than ASHPs. However, because the temperature of the ground is fairly constant at around 12°C, GSHPs have lower running costs, and are able to achieve CoPs of 4.0 or more.

3 Buildings in the relatively unusual situation of having nearby sources of water, such as lakes or rivers, may also consider water source heat pumps (WSHPs). WSHPs have a higher CoP than ASHPs but there are drawbacks around ecological sensitivities and corrosion of the heat exchangers.

As institutions in the eternity business, churches with sufficient available land should look seriously at the long-term operational and environmental benefits of GSHPs. 'Sufficient available' may narrow things down because graveyards do not make suitable candidates for GSHPs out of respect for their occupants and other archaeological remains.

One of the challenges of installing heat pumps is that rarely can they be bolted on to a pre-existing system of pipes and radiators. This is because a standard gas-fired boiler will deliver a heat flow of 65°C or more. By contrast, the CoP of heat pumps falls rapidly if they are being asked to deliver flow temperatures much above 45°C. This, in turn, means that a higher surface area of emitter is required to deliver the same amount of heat from a heat pump as from a boiler. This will add to installation costs and may require large radiators that are not ideally suited in the heritage context of many church buildings. Given this, the ideal output from a heat pump system comes through underfloor emitters. These

Air source heat pumps, discreetly located on the north roof of the chancel, Sherborne Abbey.

also represent the best solution in terms of perceptions of warmth; underfloor heating has the greatest impact around the ankles and lower legs, which are the most prone to chills from draughts.

Given the complexities of the above, a number of churches that have gone down the route of installing heat pumps have chosen not to rely on new technology alone – at least not yet. There is an option to combine heat pumps with traditional gas boilers. These so called 'bivalent' systems work in one of two ways. They take a base level of warmth from the heat pumps, but use gas either to top up the flow temperature, if the surface area of the emitters has yet to be upgraded, or to do extra work during the coldest weeks of the winter. More technology of course means that there is more to go wrong. However, bivalent systems do represent a step in the right direction. Examples of bivalent gas/ASHP systems have been installed in recent years in large ecclesiastical spaces, such as Newcastle Cathedral and Sherborne Abbey and in the smaller space of St Mary's, Beaminster in Dorset. An innovative bivalent gas and WSHP system has been introduced at Bath Abbey, tapping the unwanted heat coming from the warm outflow waters of the adjacent Roman baths.

CARBON REDUCTION

Those concerned about the aesthetics of heat pumps may be inspired by this air-conditioning unit disguised as a welcome desk, decorated with a cross: an unlikely innovation from the remote Odigìtrias Monastery in southern Crete.

My final footnote about heat pumps is that they are likely to increase the demands placed on the local electricity network. An upgrade to your supply may be needed before you can commission your heat pump system. Upgrades are not always possible; even when they are, they are rarely quick to arrive. I am aware of a couple of heat pump projects that have been delayed for months because nobody told the electricity board that more power was going to be needed.

In some contexts, there may be alternatives to heat pumps. Buildings in urban spaces will have no land for GSHPs and insufficient electricity for everyone to upgrade to ASHPs. However, urban settings make good candidates for district heating networks. This is where heat recovered from industrial use and/or generated from low-carbon sources is shared around buildings in an area. A district network is being developed in central Bristol, which may represent the low-carbon future of heating the cathedral and other buildings in the city.[11]

Lighting

Whereas heat pumps still feel very much at that 'bleeding edge' of technology, we can be more confident that lighting has firmly made the transition to low-energy solutions through the roll-out of light-emitting diodes (LEDs). Churches can invest with confidence in replacing older lighting systems with new equipment that will deliver better illumination for a fraction of the running cost.

I was rather taken aback, one Friday evening in late 2014, when a delightful and very polite parishioner called at my house to apologize for disturbing me, but did I know that the church roof was on fire? 'Umm, no,' I replied. It turned out that one of the sodium halide lamps fixed to the ceiling beams of the nave had overheated and had burst into flames. The fire brigade promptly arrived and sprayed lots of foam around, conveniently cleaning the rafters of all the dust that had built up since the lighting had been installed ten years previously.

Near disaster had been averted and, although it was a headache to be forced to address our lighting just after installing a new heating system (see p. 36), it turned out to be a blessing in disguise. We were fortunate to secure the services of a leading local company that specialized in installing LEDs in churches. After having looked at a couple of examples of their work in other churches, we knew we were in very capable hands. The system that they supplied had manifold advantages.

- First, unlike the previous system, which used unattractive industrial luminaires to flood the church floor with light, this new system carefully directed light where we needed it to go. Narrow profiled lamps were targeted at the front of the church to highlight the person who was reading the lesson or delivering a sermon. High-level lamps picked out medieval features of the building that had not been properly seen since the day they were installed centuries earlier.
- Second, the new system was controlled by a protocol called a digital addressable lighting interface (DALI). This meant that it could be operated from a simple push-button panel by the door. Behind the panel, however, was a very sophisticated system that could be accessed through a tablet, which allowed us to adjust each lamp or bank of lamps from 1 to 100 per cent of their output capacity. This enabled us to establish lighting 'scenes' for different services around

the year, which added significantly to the atmosphere during the liturgy. It also opened a new ministry for someone to control the lighting at big services – a great opportunity for teenagers who were reluctant to undertake more up-front tasks such as serving and singing.
- Third, LEDs are very reliable. One lamp unit failed within a few weeks. I am told that such early failures are not infrequent but that, once the early days are traversed, everything should be fine, with minimal maintenance for years. The broken unit was replaced for free by the company, after which the system proved faultless.
- The final advantage of our new lighting system was that it slashed our electricity bills. This turned out to be ideal timing as we were looking to make the church much more accessible through unstaffed opening (see pp. 52–60).

LEDs consume as little as a tenth of the power needed to run older incandescent and halide systems. The money saved in terms of electricity means that relamping from old lighting to LEDs is likely to pay for itself over the lifespan of a system. Lower electricity bills mean a lower carbon footprint. Even if you are on a green tariff, reducing your electricity consumption means that more electricity generated from renewable sources is available in the grid for use by others, since the National Grid is less reliant on generating power from gas-burning power stations.

By relamping St Michael's, St Albans, with LEDs in 2015, we felt as if we were taking a risk on the cutting-edge of lighting technology. Ten years down the line, LEDs are a proven technology. Salisbury Cathedral has recently been relamped with LEDs, a process that has slashed our electricity bill by tens of thousands of pounds and our carbon footprint by 30 tonnes or more of CO_2 a year.

If you are thinking of installing LEDs in your church, here are a few headlines that you should consider, alongside the support that you will get from your architect and DAC.

- Stay in control of your professional agents. Do you need a new lighting system or are you just looking to replace the lamps? Try to avoid the need to design a whole new system if you can. If you are happy with the layout of your existing lamps and can reuse the previous power cables, you will save on installation costs and avoid being drawn into long and costly conversations with lighting companies about design work. Hopefully, this solution would also minimize or even eradicate the need for any new drilling: this would be best for the care of your building and should ease the passage of your proposal through the faculty process.

- The international (SI) unit of illumination is the lux. Seek advice about how much lux you need for the functions of your building. The lux needed in pews for reading will differ from the requirements in your porch for safe egress. This is also an access issue because those with impaired sight will benefit from higher levels of lux – but not glare.

- In a similar vein, the 'temperature' of colour is measured in kelvins (K). Historic buildings benefit from a 'warm white' so, if you are installing lamps with only one colour, aim for 2700–3000K. As colour temperature heads towards 4000K, it becomes a harsh 'cold blue'. But if you drop towards 2000K (candlelight), things can become rather gloomy. Full-colour LEDs are also available, but these units are generally bulkier and may have a shorter lifespan. Also, they may not deliver adequate bang for the extra buck compared with lamps that only emit a fixed temperature of white light.

- Think about control systems. The DALI installed in St Michael's, St Albans, is a typical control system for heritage buildings. Digital Multiplex (DMX) is an alternative wired control system, but it is more common in theatres and sports arenas. Wireless controls (e.g. Casambi) work by relaying the control signal from lamp to lamp. Inevitably, wireless controls are cheaper but need to be researched with care because signals can get blocked by the thick walls and heavy pillars that are typical in many churches.

- Think long term in order to maximize savings. The industry standard is that an LED lamp will last for 50K hours. This does not mean that after 50K hours a unit will suddenly drop dead. It means that after 50K hours, the average unit will work at up to 70 per cent of its original maximum capacity. In other words, the units fade away as individual LED chips within each lamp wear out. With this in mind it is worth installing enough lamps so that you do not have to run each lamp at 100 per cent capacity; if they are not maxed out, they will last longer and give you a bit of bunce if you need to crank them up towards the end of their lifespan.

Solar power and batteries

Solar power is a very visible form of low-carbon technology and so can be put on a pedestal as the immediate solution for carbon reduction. The technology has also come a long way, generating more power through units that last longer and look considerably more attractive than they once did. So solar panels have a vital role to play in the future global energy mix. My only caution is that photovoltaic (PV) cells may not represent the lowest hanging fruit, as you seek to reduce your carbon footprint. Do the maths. If you have yet to relamp your church with LEDs, you are likely to save more money and carbon by prioritizing the renewal of your lighting system over the installation of solar panels.

As with all the projects considered in this chapter, there is excellent advice about planning for the installation of PV cells on the net zero playlist of the Church Care YouTube channel.[12] This talks through the best places on your building for generating solar power; the structural engineering considerations of installing PV panels on your roof; how the equipment can be connected to the rest of your electrical system; navigating the pitfalls of the permission process; and issues of whether to retain the electricity on site or add it to the National Grid.

Solar panels on Salisbury Cathedral.

Solar panels will be increasingly useful in those contexts where they can be combined with battery storage. This will allow power that is generated on sunny days to be retained and used on site at times of the day and year when less solar energy is available. However, several recent accidents have exposed fire safety concerns around large batteries. Even so, battery technology is improving rapidly, so more may be possible for less space and lower costs in future years. Given this, if you are installing PV panels, think hard about whether you also want batteries at this stage or whether it makes more sense to future-proof your system. Doing so would mean allowing space and providing connectors so that batteries could be added to the system in the future. For example, the plans of Salisbury Cathedral to create a carbon neutral office block, which went to planning in 2024, include a substantial ground array of solar panels. We considered supporting this with battery storage but decided that this was not yet right for us. Instead, we chose to leave space in the design of the outhouses, where batteries could potentially be added further down the line.

The most helpful insight I have ever had into the cost-benefit profile of solar panels came through a former parishioner, Marjorie. Marjorie was truly a gentlewoman and had risen to the vaunted status of being the oldest member of our congregation in St Albans. But in no way did this mean she had a traditional outlook. When it came to new technology, Marjorie was always an early adopter. Shortly after I arrived in the parish in 2012, Marjorie and I were having our first proper conversation – but she cut it short because she said that she had to go and Skype her daughter in California. I had literally no idea what she was talking about. A similar story was told at her funeral about an incident, from the mid 2000s, when Marjorie had been confronted on her doorstep by a solar-panel salesman. Erroneously identifying Marjorie as a soft target, the man recited his predictable patter about the benefits of installing the wonderful new panels that he was peddling. Marjorie cut him dead by saying that she was 80; she shrewdly enquired when a customer might expect a return on their investment. Thrown onto the back foot, the salesman looked rather sheepish and announced that the payback time was about ten years. 'You're on,' said Marjorie. She won her gamble by more than five years.

CARBON REDUCTION

Getting on the right side of history

There are many other ways in which your church can witness to the fifth Mark of Mission (see p. 91) and reduce its carbon footprint.

- The above opportunities about heating, lighting, solar power and batteries are equally applicable if your church is fortunate to own any other property, such as a hall or a house.
- It might be worth reviewing your consumables. Does your church office use recycled products whenever possible? Do you know the food miles of items in your kitchen? What are the carbon credentials of your main contractors?
- Likewise disposals. Does rubbish from your site go to landfill or can you secure a contract with one of the clever refuse companies that separate and recycle as much waste as they can?
- Do you seek to use public transport when possible? I was delighted when Salisbury Cathedral's choir recently revised its plans for a European tour, changing from air travel to going by train, a much greener solution.
- Don't forget about inbuilt carbon. All your buildings will have consumed energy at the time when they were raised; current techniques for the production of concrete are particularly carbon intensive. Can you minimize future changes to these buildings and so maximize the benefits of the embedded carbon to reduce the environmental implications of fresh construction?
- Possibilities for your church grounds will be considered in the next chapter, including EV charging points in car parks and rewilding your churchyard.

As a critical mission issue, carbon reduction is not just about what we do as a church. It naturally feeds into the messages that we share with our congregations, through liturgy, preaching, prayer and music. Do you use the seasons of the year, the Church calendar or Scripture to teach and pray about environmental themes? Are you making connections between the steps that you are taking as a church to reduce your carbon footprint and the ways in which this resonates with the global agenda of climate change and the everyday lives of those in your congregation? It is essential that churches are seen to be putting their own houses in order; but in tandem with this, we will have an even bigger impact if we can enable our worshippers to live out the same principles in their homes, and advocate for carbon reduction in their places of work and neighbourhoods.

The principle of animating the whole congregation is fundamental to the Eco Church scheme of A Rocha UK.[13] Eco Church is described as

> a learning community of churches of all shapes and sizes. It provides a framework to support your church and its leadership to take practical action on caring for God's earth. It includes a toolkit of resources, an online award survey, a quarterly email update, online events, prayer forums and occasional conferences.[14]

For many congregations, the Eco Church bronze, silver and gold awards are the gateway to grappling with environmental issues. I mention Eco Church late in this chapter only because it is a summary of so much of what this chapter is about: building a systemic approach that embodies, in local faith communities, what needs to be achieved across the whole globe.

At the end of the day, there are few easy or cheap solutions for decarbonization, including in our churches. As scientists have come to understand climate change better, the stark truth has emerged that generations have benefited from cheap energy because the cost of using fossil fuels has never included the true price of consumption – that is, the cost of long-term damage to the atmosphere of our planet. The grim reality is that we're going to have to pay more for our energy in the future, in addition to which the cost of resilience to climate change will only grow if we procrastinate about making the transition to green technologies. This creates massive issues of intergenerational equity as well as the social injustice already noted. Difficult though it will be politically, we need cross-party consensus and international agreements to nudge individuals and institutions to decarbonize as quickly as possible. Prompt decarbonization has to be combined with an equally unpalatable rebalancing of the tax system, away from the older generations that have enjoyed the unpriced benefits of carbon consumption and towards the younger generation that must tackle the unwitting consequences of their forebears' actions.

The need for churches to get onto the front foot is urgent. A parallel may be drawn with the way in which churches responded to the injustices of slavery two centuries ago. Back then, some Christians colluded with the system of cheap energy that came in the form of slave labour, either because they failed to see an injustice that was integral to the imperial societies of the day, or because they thought the problem was too big to tackle. History rightly looks back at such complacency with stern judgement and searching calls for research, reflection and reparation. Reversing the telescope of history, I can see equivalent legacy issues coming down the line in a hundred years' time around climate change denial. Those who today downplay the enormity or even the reality of the issue, or who drag their heels in the implementation of solutions, will be regarded with the same disdain as the slavers of yesteryear. So the missional opportunities for Christians to speak into these issues is very considerable. However, we will need to tackle our own carbon emissions if we are to earn the right to address this issue with a prophetic authority that flows from our understanding that the world is God's gift to us and our great-grandchildren.

Notes

1 https://www.vatican.va/content/francesco/en/encyclicals/documents/papa-francesco_20150524_enciclica-laudato-si.html (accessed 12.3.25).

2 *The Bishops' Letter about the Climate*, 2020, 2nd edn, The Church of Sweden, at https://www.svenskakyrkan.se/a-bishops-letter-about-the-climate (accessed 12.3.25).

3 https://www.anglicancommunion.org/mission/marks-of-mission.aspx (accessed 12.3.25).

4 https://www.churchofengland.org/sites/default/files/2022-06/nzc_2030_routemap_june22.pdf (accessed 12.3.25).

5 https://www.churchofengland.org/resources/churchcare (accessed 12.3.25).

6 https://www.youtube.com/playlist?list=PLZwBculXCbbPI9X-z7WvEav03waUzzjBcv

7 https://historicengland.org.uk/services-skills/training-skills/training/webinars/technical-tuesdays (accessed 12.3.25).

8 https://historicengland.org.uk/images-books/publications/adapting-historic-buildings-energy-carbon-efficiency-advice-note-18 (accessed 12.3.25).

9 https://parishbuying.org.uk (accessed 12.3.25).

10 https://www.nationalgrid.com/deliveringfor2035 (accessed 12.3.25).

11 https://bristol-cathedral.co.uk/about-us/sustainability (accessed 12.3.25).

12 https://www.youtube.com/playlist?list=PLZwBculXCbbPI9X-z7WvEav03waUzzjBcv (accessed 12.3.25).

13 https://arocha.org.uk (accessed 12.3.25).

14 https://arocha.org.uk/what-we-do/eco-church (accessed 12.3.25).

6

Churchyards: From untamed jungles to sacred ground

Throughout this book, we have been seeing how 'church' as building can be a means by which newcomers encounter 'church' as people. By extension, where a church building is surrounded by green space, the churchyard has a role to play in that process, as worshippers and visitors step onto holy ground. How churchyards are maintained and used will have much to say about the values and views of a congregation concerning inclusion and welcome, as much as about the environment and heritage. In addition to graveyards, local churches may also own other parcels of land, such as car parks and gardens. This chapter will therefore examine the considerable challenges of land management for church leaders; it will also explore how these challenges can be mitigated, before outlining some specific suggestions of ways in which church grounds can be used for missional purposes or financial benefit.

Requiem aeternam?

We should begin with a reality check: churchyards present a whole host of headaches on top of those that come from running a place of worship.

First, they are a health and safety nightmare. Churchyards that are poorly maintained will be riddled with crumbling walls and tottering gravestones. Looming trees may threaten to drop branches onto visitors and leaves into gutters; they may send out roots that crack pathways and turn them into dangerous trip hazards. The ground itself may be pitted with mole hills and badger holes. These problems can all impair access to the church, especially for those with limited sight and mobility.

Second, the size and maintenance of churchyards are likely to create issues around security and safeguarding. Low levels of lighting can attract antisocial behaviour. Depending on the context, this can take the form of littering, dog mess, drunkenness, drug-taking, unsolicited camping and even protest gatherings.

Some of these problems can be compounded by overgrown shrubbery. The problem with most plants is that they change slower than human memory. Everybody notices when plants are cut back and some will complain. But year-on-year growth is hard to spot – we just assume it has always looked that way. Only when compared to historical photos can we see the impact of ever-increasing amounts of foliage. The upshot of unchecked growth is what I have heard described as 'rapey bushes': the sort of unwanted shrubbery that makes people feel unsafe, especially at night. Rapey bushes have the added potential to make your church or hall less visible to passers-by in a way that facilitates damage or burglary.

Third, the function of churchyards as places of burial can pose a potent emotional hurdle for many. Too many gothic horror movies have been set in the half light of fog-laced graveyards. Scenes with zombies and ghouls make for popular cinema but do not promote the gospel message about death as a horizon of peace and hope.

By way of illustration, here's an example from personal experience: one misty autumn Sunday morning when I was a vicar, the churchwarden and I were opening up for an 8 a.m. service. We discovered a couple filming in the churchyard. The man was directing a sophisticated-looking camera onto the woman, who was pretending to claw her way out of the ground from behind a tombstone. She was clad only in a thin wedding dress and had a faceless flesh-coloured mask over her head. I was amused and concerned in roughly equal measure. The couple claimed they were working on a short movie as part of their course at the local college. A stiff email was subsequently despatched to the head of film studies, with whom I later had an amicable conversation. We discussed the advice that the college gives to students as regards filming on church property, and procedures for seeking permission.

Beyond such populist misconceptions of churchyards as haunted places, graveyards may present a more a deep-seated and theological challenge. Historically, Christians have buried their dead around churches for thoroughly positive reasons. Unlike ancient Greek necropoli (literally, 'cities of the dead') the Christian 'cemetery' means, etymologically, a place of 'sleep'. This is a wholly different and more optimistic image. If cemeteries are places where the dead are sleeping, when we come to worship, we are joining our praises with those of our departed loved ones, whose souls rejoice around God's throne in heaven. Christian worship is thus an anticipation of the resurrection of the dead: the hope of all God's saints.

I suspect that many Christians have forgotten this last point – or have never quite believed it. However, the effect of downplaying the doctrine of the resurrection of the dead is to turn cemeteries from places of hopeful sleeping, from whence we will one day rise again – whatever that may look like! – into places of permanence. Ultimate permanence. And if the places where we leave our dead are perceived as ultimately permanent, they become places where nothing is allowed to change. I have come across several instances of an individual's reluctance to agree to modest proposals to develop one or other aspect of their church or churchyard. Such reluctance is subconsciously bound up with their experience of bereavement, loss and trauma, and the presence of a loved one's remains in the vicinity. A false syllogism can present itself; it proceeds from the truth that the dead are dead, and there is nothing more we can do for them, to arrive at the error that says the place where the dead are buried should be perpetually unchanging.

A combination of the above issues about safety, security and spirituality creates two particular challenges for those charged with managing churchyards. First, they can be a big financial liability. Churchyards are costly to maintain. And the return on investment (be that in money or volunteer time) can be meagre. The plants keep growing and the walls keep crumbling. Second, churchyards are a toxic prospect when it comes to marketing. Who in their right mind would want to come to a building if they have to pass through a graveyard first? (The only silver lining I have discovered is that nobody knocks on the vicarage door at Halloween to trick or treat if they must first walk through the churchyard. But what about the other 364 days of the year?) Are there ways in which we can make churchyards a little more inviting by transforming their challenges into opportunities?

It is essential that we get right the physical approach to our places of worship. Nigel Walter stresses the role played by churchyards as the soft edge of a church. He writes that they can act as an 'initial zone of engagement' between a congregation and members of the public. 'If well-managed, this threshold space will convey a sense of welcome and of being open to making friends' (Walter, 2014, pp. 6, 7). As a priest I am also conscious of the natural meditative quality of churchyards. They are places that invite us to slow down, to breathe in fresh air, and to think about the big things in life. Often when waiting outside a church on a significant occasion, a line from John Betjeman's poem 'Saint Cadoc' pops into my head. It is about how newly married couples walk along the same sacred paths over which the coffins of the dead are carried on other occasions (Betjeman, p. 81). This is not a Hollywood pastiche of the dead, but a reminder that churchyards are places in which the full circle of life is present. The seriousness of churchyards can draw us away from trivia and towards reflection. Similar to Betjeman, an earlier poet, John Donne, explored on several occasions the significance of doorways and the imagery of crossing thresholds. He sets the scene of his 'Hymn to God in my sickness' by imagining that he is outside God's throne room. But he might as readily have imagined himself in a cemetery, pondering the entrance of a church.

> Since I am coming to that holy room,
>   Where, with thy choir of saints for evermore,
> I shall be made thy music; as I come
>   I tune the instrument here at the door,
>   And what I must do then, think now before. (Donne, pp. 610–11)

To me, these thought-provoking verses are a reminder that there is huge pastoral and spiritual potential in churchyards, if only we can get over the molehills in order to discover the holy mountain.

Minimizing liabilities

The place to start with managing a churchyard is to find out who is responsible for what. This is a simple 'open and closed' question. Ironic though it sounds, churchyards that are 'closed' can be maintained in at least as welcoming a fashion as those that are 'open'.

Legally, 'open' churchyards are those that still have space for fresh burials of coffins in new plots of land. However, once all the land is used up, a PCC can apply to the Privy Council for the churchyard to be 'closed'. Once a churchyard has been closed by an Order in Council, responsibility for its maintenance passes from the PCC to the local authority. This obscure rule was enshrined in the Burial Act 1855 and subsequent local authority legislation. The rationale behind the law is that, during such time as a churchyard can receive fresh burials, the principal beneficiaries of the land are the congregation; this is because they can be buried in the land and the church can derive an income from burial fees. However, once the land is full, the benefit of the space can be enjoyed only by members of the public who pass through for recreational purposes, and that they do so equally, whatever their faith tradition or none – hence the law, which shifts responsibility to the local authority that provides services for all residents within its district.

It goes without saying that your local authority will not be a fan of closed churchyards. This is because they represent a liability to the council taxpayer. For churches, however, the Burial Act 1855 is their friend. A priest I know was horrified to discover that the parish of which he had just become vicar was paying several thousand pounds a year to maintain a churchyard that should have been closed decades earlier. He initiated the process of closure through the Privy Council and promptly saved his church a hefty annual bill.

The added joy of the Burial Act 1855 is that, while closing a churchyard shifts responsibility for maintenance of the land to the local authority, the church retains ownership. This means that the church can keep burying ashes, even after its yard is closed to fresh burials by an Order in Council. The reason for this is that families pay the church to lease a plot in which a coffin is buried, but such is not the case in a garden of remembrance; with regard to ashes, the church retains ownership of the land and does not derive burial income from the land itself.

The Burial Act 1855 played out to the advantage of the parish where I served in St Albans in several respects. During my decade in the parish, the local authority helpfully paid for intermittent one-off works, including repairs to the tarmacked drive through the yard, repointing the perimeter walls, and surveying and carrying out surgery on a number of trees. The council taxpayer benefited from this investment in the form of a beautiful green space, which many residents enjoyed.

Furthermore, before my time, the PCC had cut a deal to undertake routine maintenance on behalf of the local authority in return for an annual grant. A churchyard team dealt with the weeding and mowing. This resulted in a win-win: the churchyard was much better maintained than if the council had bought in professional services, and the PCC was paid a fee that covered the servicing and depreciation of our ride-on mower and other equipment.

The one downside of having a closed churchyard I found is that the local authority inevitably did not want to spend a penny more than necessary. Thus, in late 2018 when part of the churchyard wall was deemed to be leaning dangerously towards the adjacent road, the officer of the council spent many months denying that the Burial Act 1855 extended as far as rendering the council liable for the expensive repair that was needed on the perimeter wall. When, eventually, the council's solicitor advised that this was exactly what the Burial Act required, the council officers changed tack. They argued that the lean of the wall was caused by an enlarged tree in a neighbouring property, so the cost should be borne by the neighbour. At this point, the PCC was able to stand back and leave the council and the neighbour to reach an agreement. This ensured that the issue consumed only a minimal amount of bandwidth at PCC meetings. However, the agreement did result in unsightly Herras fencing around a substantial section of our wall. Moreover, it would be the church that would take the reputational hit if the wall ever collapsed because of delays in the parties reaching an agreement: regrettably, the general public are little-apprised about the finer points of the duties conferred under the Burial Act 1855.

St Michael's, St Albans, was most fortunate to have a willing band of regular and occasional churchyard helpers; the cemetery was of such a size that they could undertake routine maintenance. Not every church is so lucky. A nearby church with a closed churchyard had a congregation of a similar size, However, their cemetery was much bigger – too big for them to manage with unpaid assistance alone. Given this, they had to come to an arrangement with the local authority to target the council's annual budget for maintaining the most visible and high traffic areas of the churchyard; the more distant reaches received only minimal attention. Diplomatic skills may be needed if you are seeking a partnership with your local authority to achieve an arrangement that does the best by all stakeholders.

Review, plan and manage

The prioritization seen in this latest example serves to summarize my advice for those churchyards that remain open and where full responsibility for maintenance falls on the church. If you have an open churchyard, think about those spaces that need to be kept tidiest. This will probably be the lines of sight and approach to the building. As in Chapter 3, when thinking about welcome (p. 56), walk the route and consider what it would be like for someone who is unfamiliar with the site. Is it comfortable? Can you see clearly where you are going? Is the route overgrown and oppressive, or open and inviting? Do these feelings differ if you repeat the walk at night or in twilight?

During a walking inspection such as this, a number of issues might be identified that need attention. Document them and think about which should be prioritized. Are there any quick wins to improve the look and feel of the place? Can systems be put in place to address the medium-term issues across a couple of years? Are there longer-term projects that will need preparation and planning?

Issues identified by your churchyard review may include one or more of the following concerns.

What is the state of your pathways? Do they need clearing of weeds? Are there any trip hazards such as tree roots or lifting tarmac? Sometimes paths are made of relaid gravestones; these can become slippery from moss and may need treatment with a proprietary cleaner. Particular consideration should be given to people with access requirements, especially along the route to the church door. Is the path wide enough for users of wheelchairs? Are there any drain covers in which wheelchairs or walking sticks might get stuck?

What about levels of lighting? Initially, this should be a consideration of natural light – at night as much as during the day. Are there any of those burgeoning bushes that need cutting back? If pruning is necessary, remember to schedule it for the correct time of year for the plant in question, and in a season when birds are not nesting. Once a pruning regime is in place, consideration might be given to whether artificial lighting is necessary. External floodlighting on the church itself will go some way to illuminating the churchyard; but it will be ineffective if you have a long pathway. There are umpteen bollard-based solutions that might meet this requirement. These need not be hard-wired because some are driven by batteries and powered via a solar panel. How tough would you like your bollards to be? Should they be vandal-proof? Another consideration is the type and direction of light. Bollards should direct light down towards the ground and not outwards; this will reduce glare, which is better for the partially sighted and for wildlife. Lamps with a nice, low colour temperature (in the warm white range of 2700–3000K) are ideal, as well as being sympathetic to heritage contexts. The helpful *Dark skies of the North Wessex Downs: a guide to good external lighting* produced by the North Wessex Downs Area of Outstanding Natural Beauty documents how you can help to protect dark skies.[1]

Moving beyond the immediate pathways, it is time to consider the larger trees in your churchyard. These are likely to be subject to Tree Preservation Orders. There will be further restrictions if your churchyard is in a conservation area. Seek advice from your local authority tree officer for more information. Trees need regular inspection by a suitably qualified and licensed arboriculturist (a local authority responsibility, of course, if your churchyard is closed). The frequency of inspection will depend on the location of the tree. Those in low traffic areas may not need attention more than every three years. Trees in areas with a higher footfall (e.g. along paths or adjacent to the church itself) may need an annual check. Your insurer may have recommendations.

Tree surgery is not cheap. Establishing a regular cycle of inspection and maintenance is the best way to spread the bill. It might be possible to reduce the costs of tree surgery if you ask to have the logs left on site; however, do take care about disposal because 'wet wood' cannot be sold in the UK if the logs have a moisture content of more than 20 per cent.

Given that trees are such a mixed blessing, you might want to establish a policy about replacements and new plantings. On the plus side, trees absorb carbon dioxide; so churches with a significant number of mature trees will make decent inroads into their carbon footprint (see Chapter 5, p. 94). On the downside, trees are a liability in terms of maintenance costs. Sadly, these costs will be high compared to the environmental benefits. It takes 40 mature trees a whole year to absorb a single tonne of carbon dioxide. This means that there are probably more cost-effective ways of reducing your carbon footprint than planting more trees in your churchyard.

Moving beyond the trees, are there any other structures in your churchyard? What state are they in?

- If you have sheds, are they locked and well maintained? Due consideration should be given to the safe storage of tools and chemicals, including fuel.
- What is the state of your perimeter wall, hedge or fence? Are there any leaning or deteriorated sections? Should these be cordoned off, pending repair?
- If you have any benches, are they still fit for purpose or have they rotted through? And where are they located? Benches in the right places are a blessing to the visitor. Benches in the wrong places can catalyse antisocial behaviour or just be ignored. There are sometimes sensitivities around benches that have been given *in memoriam*. Flipping this, the perennial interest in memorial benches is such that you may be able to establish a list of potential donors to replace seats as they cease to be fit for purpose.
- And how about your gravestones? It is good practice to give these an annual 'wobble test'. For the sake of safety, any leaning, cracked or loose stones should be laid flat to the ground. Within the Church of England, responsibility for memorials on a grave rests with the family; but there may come times when families are unable or unwilling to maintain these. Further advice may be found in your diocesan churchyard regulations or from the diocesan registrar.
- Finally, what about the ground itself? Is there any unsightly waste, especially detritus left from antisocial behaviour, that could usefully be tidied away? Remember that your churchyard is your shop window. Are there any holes in high-traffic areas that need filling? Take care not to block holes that are actively occupied by animals.

Given the nature of a graveyard, it is not uncommon to find the bereaved leaving tributes to lost loved ones. These can be attractive and touching. To the person who left them, they are likely to be heartfelt tokens. To the dispassionate onlooker, they may become an eyesore. Floral tributes soon wilt. Trinkets become litter, especially if plastic. Large mementos may represent a private imposition on a shared space. All this means that you may need to take a policy decision about how to manage such artefacts, especially in busier areas of the churchyard. Given the sensitivities involved, this will need careful communication. If you would like to avoid using signage that says 'no' or 'don't', you may wish to consider what subtle messages are given to families at the time of interment.

Or could you nudge the process, for example, by creating a memorial area with fixed pots for floral tributes, on the understanding that older posies will be cleared away on a regular basis? Or could you designate one tree, with low-hanging branches, on which collated tributes might be hung?

Finally, given the nature of a graveyard, you should be ready for those times when pieces of bone work their way through to the surface. Bones should be promptly removed or covered because some find them unnerving, especially the young. The general rule of thumb is that individual bones or fragments should be reverently gathered and reburied in an appropriate corner of the yard. However, in the less likely scenario that you discover any articulated bones (more than one bone joined together), you should consult an archaeologist.

Go wild?

If everything discussed above sounds like hard work and a distraction from other tasks, maybe you should consider rewilding. Paradoxically, this is a way of doing more for less. Rewilding comes in different forms and has the principal benefit of fostering biodiversity.

Passive rewilding can be achieved by leaving sections of your graveyard to go fallow. By not mowing areas of grass, wildflowers will flourish; these provide seasonal colour and support bees and other pollinators, which are vital for flourishing ecosystems. To keep things manageable, rewilded grass still needs an autumn trim once the plant life has died back; but that is a single cut and not as expensive as regular mowing throughout the summer. Another version of the same principle is to adopt a less intensive management approach to your hedges. Are there sections of hedge that could be less frequently cut on the tops and/or sides? This approach can create space in which birds and small mammals find shelter for nesting or food to eat.

It is possible to build on the success of passive rewilding through the active introduction of particular species. I'm not thinking here about boars and beavers; more the deliberate sowing of mixed wildflower seeds. Care should be taken, when selecting the mix, that the seeds are appropriate for your soil and weather conditions. It is likely that a rewilded area will take several seasons of growth and natural pollination for full diversity to be achieved. Lots of advice about managing grassland and connecting people with nature is available on the website of Plantlife.[2]

In addition to plants, diversity of wildlife can be encouraged through the introduction of nesting boxes for birds or small mammals in appropriate locations. Your compost heap is already likely to be a de facto bug hotel. Further advice and resources about managing your churchyard for ecological gain may be found on the website of the conservation charity known as Caring for God's Acre.[3]

Not everyone is a fan of rewilding. Some people think it leaves land looking scruffy and prone to the problems of overgrowth and disuse. But there is a difference between carefully managed rewilding and disorganized neglect.

Tensions between the different approaches to rewilding played out in St Albans. The medieval church, St Michael's, chose to adopt a more intensive approach to churchyard management. Principally, this was to tame a corner of the churchyard that had become inaccessible because of too many nettles. We chose to cut back the nettles because we needed that part of the yard to be available for children to play after services, and for occasional functions held outside – of which more shortly. By contrast, oversight of the grounds at the smaller church, St Mary's, was in the hands of a parishioner who had a passion for rewilding. St Mary's was a quieter site and so we adopted a policy of leaving the grass in front of the church to grow, while maintaining a managed and welcoming pathway between the road and the porch. Both solutions were appropriate to their context: there is a balance to be struck.

If your church is unsure about rewilding, one way to test the waters is to support 'No Mow May'. This widely recognized initiative does exactly what it says on the tin: grassed areas are left uncut during a crucial month in the spring for rejuvenating plants and nesting birds. As a temporary measure, the scheme can be introduced across all or some of your churchyard; it will not create a permanently scruffy area because a prior cut can be done in late April. No Mow May is also a simple principle that can be promoted to congregations as something to try at home if they have gardens with lawns.

There are two final issues to bear in mind when considering a wildflower area in your churchyard. First, think about topography. What goes on in each section of your churchyard? If, for example, one corner

Wildflower planting, Salisbury Cathedral.

is busier than others as a site of active burials and where people come to visit the graves of recently deceased loved ones, it will be important to maintain good access through mown pathways. By contrast, more historic and disused sections, especially those away from footpaths and the church itself, may be ideal for rewilding.

Second, having designated your wildflower area, it is useful to add some simple but clear signage to explain what is going on. This allows the casual visitor to understand that the area is being purposefully managed and not wantonly abandoned. It also allows you to set the theological tone: 'At St Tiddlywinks, we're doing our bit to care for God's planet by leaving this area unmown to promote colourful biodiversity and wildlife,' or something similar.

Outdoor worship

Rewilding and No Mow May are examples of ways in which churches that are on top of their churchyards can start to use them constructively: to promote gently the values and message of the gospel and to further the ministry of the congregation. There are many other creative projects that may assist your mission and/or defray the costs of managing your land.

Churchyards can be used for worship, prayer and teaching, either on a temporary or permanent basis. One of the unanticipated consequences of the coronavirus restrictions was that churches had to think creatively about how they might get together when they began to meet again for worship in person. Congregations with outdoor space suddenly found themselves blessed with ready access to an area in which they could gather. Also, outdoor services inadvertently brought them closer to their local communities. Instead of being huddled inside a building, worship was vulnerably exposed to those passing by. This dramatically lowered the bar that outsiders needed to clear in order to join an act of worship. It was a missional learning point from which churches can continue to benefit.

Outdoor worship presents all sorts of challenges about access, seating, music, toilets and so on, most of which can be overcome with a little forethought and preparation. But there are also great opportunities to do things more creatively outside than inside a familiar building.[4] For example, service themes could tap into the inherent spirituality of the context and season, such as a pet blessing near the time of the feast of St Francis (4 October) or starlit carols in December. In addition, unlike during the coronavirus restrictions, churches are now permitted the Plan B of retreating inside should the weather turn out to be bad.

Churchyards are not only great for gathered worship; they also provide places for private prayer and contemplation. Churches can encourage this by thinking about the prompts and resources that could be made available around their site.

Given that your churchyard is likely to be frequently visited by those who are mourning the death of loved ones or researching the history of the more-distantly deceased, it naturally serves as a place where people reflect on the big things of life. You can support this latent spirituality by how you position seating, especially within any garden of remembrance. Tasteful signage can extend words of comfort and support. In the digital age, online links to further resources, information about the life of the local church or pastoral support can be made available through QR codes.

Further opportunities may present themselves around the seasons of the year. Through them you might foster prayer and reflection in your churchyard. Some churches have outside crib scenes at Christmas or Easter gardens in celebration of the Resurrection. These can be accompanied by invitational signage, explaining the story and directing the reader to where they can find out more. If it is the tradition of your church to use stations of the cross, could these be taken into the churchyard, either for prayer with a group or for individual use by those walking through? Ideally, the theme of each station might link to its location. Do you have a stone pavement to echo the judgement seat of Pilate (John 19.13) or a higher bit of ground that could recall the hill of Calvary? A similar opportunity presents itself at Eastertide with the more recent custom of stations of the Resurrection (*Common Worship: times and seasons*, pp. 443–68). In addition to stations that reflect the liturgical season, other churches have developed prayer stations that are more thematic. Lots of creative ideas are available online, for example from Engage Worship.[5]

Building the Easter Garden: all-age worship on Good Friday, St Michael's, St Albans.

Outdoor gathering

Bearing in mind Nigel Walter's words about threshold spaces (see pp. 56 and 115), might there be other beneficial uses of your sacred space, in addition to the overtly spiritual activities outlined above? Historically, churchyards served as focal points for gathering and jollity. Churches are rediscovering these sorts of traditions by hosting events such as charitable fetes and beer festivals. Care needs to be taken not to distract or offend the more contemplative. However, when done tastefully, these events can have a significant impact on how a church is perceived within the local community.

One of the biggest opportunities in the life of St Michael's, St Albans, was the annual Folk Night in early July. Historically, this celebration of music and dance took place along the street from the church. However, when a local pub closed down, its car park was no longer available as a venue for one of the bands. We invited the band to relocate to the churchyard. We were initially cautious because of the potential noise and disruption. However, the first year went really well: the weather proved kind, the band loved the relaxed venue, there was plenty of space on the grass for the audience to sit and listen, and families felt that their children were safe within the confines of the churchyard walls.

Building on this success, we sought to develop our involvement in subsequent years. Entry to Folk Night was always free; but we decided that we could monetize our involvement by selling refreshments. Our Mission and Community committee organized a stall selling wine and soft drinks, and we franchised other stands. One went to a local brewery to serve its beer. Others sold food: one year there was a hog roast; the next there was a Caribbean kitchen, accompanied by an ice-cream stand run by a nearby café. The end result was a decent sum to donate to the band for their efforts and the remainder went into the parish funds.

The most important thing about Folk Night was that it broke down false perceptions about the church and its congregation. It told the community that we were open for people like them. Again and again, we'd hear comments such as 'It's great to see you're involved in Folk Night' or 'I never knew St Michael's did something like this'. It was the day in the year when we saw more people than any other. There were literally hundreds passing through the churchyard within the course of a few short hours. I had many pastoral conversations over a beer or two. And,

Folk Night at St Michael's, St Albans.

after a few cautious early years, we chose to open the church during Folk Night, staffed with regular worshippers. Doing so allowed us to engage many who had never crossed the threshold of our porch before.

The connections made through Folk Night were palpable. Inevitably, the festival was sadly cancelled in 2020 by the coronavirus restrictions. However, one evening in July that year I was wandering through the churchyard and saw the band, sitting on the grass. They explained that it was the night when the festival should have taken place – I had completely forgotten – and they had decided to meet up as a small group. They said that Folk Night was their best gig in the year and they longed for a return to normality. I was moved to tears.

I had been equally touched a few years earlier when a local poet, John Mole, wrote a poem about the festival and the church's involvement in it. His lines distilled – as only good verse can – the significance of the event for so many. John's words were so fitting that he allowed us to blow them up onto a large banner. We hung it, during Folk Night, on the east end of the church to greet festivalgoers as they came into the churchyard.

> Shadows there on the flint wall,
> Ink-black silhouettes much
> Larger than in life, reach
> Out to each other. Who can tell

That light is not playing tricks
Or that a well-aimed beam
Has not now usurped the moon
And the hands of the church clock

Gone into reverse? These
Could all be ghosts relieved
Of their whiteness, the loved,
The lost, returned to praise

This annual gathering –
Stranger, neighbour, friend
Who wander on sacred ground
To drink and dance and sing.
(John Mole, 2020, p. 33; reproduced by kind permission)

Beyond the spiritual and social, churchyards also have great educational potential. Gravestones are a timeless resource for historians who wish to research the 'rude forefathers' of the hamlet.[6] Churchyards can also be used by schools to teach about, maybe, the history of those who are buried in the space, about natural science or even materials engineering. Classes from the local primary school would occasionally pop into St Michael's churchyard to learn about plants and animals. There were occasions in the summer when Children's Church used the yard on Sundays for a mixture of fun and reflection on God's creation.

Outdoor other

Not all church land is full of bodies and ashes. The agricultural assets of the Church of England were centralized in the 1970s, when parishes' 'glebe' came under the direct administration of the dioceses. Glebe is part of the historic income of the parish clergy of England; it continues to contribute towards stipends. Some glebe land may still be available for use by parishes. Prudent dioceses take into account local interests when arranging leases and sales. Our parish, for example, had permission from the principal user of its glebe, the local primary school, to organize occasional family and youth gatherings, and also a big bonfire in November.

Other than the glebe, churches may have other parcels of land that they can use for gospel purposes. My former church of St Mary's, Childwick Green, had been bequeathed a quarter of an acre by a major local landowner in the late twentieth century. The land had been leased by the parish as an extension of an adjacent private garden. It returned, however, to direct management by the parish when the lease concluded, during my time as vicar. On initial glance, this land looked like a liability, with trees to maintain and a lawn to mow. However, it proved an excellent venue for worship (e.g. the annual Animal Service) and socials, such as parish barbecues. The garden could also be hired out alongside the church's Schoolroom for small-scale parties. We even earned a modest one-off fee for installing a communications mast on the site, with the reputational bonus that we could claim we were bringing superfast broadband to the village. Around the other side of St Albans, St Mary's, Marshalswick, has transformed a disused parcel of land adjacent to the church into a community garden project: Peppercorn Place. Fruit and vegetables are grown for the needy; the space also offers a quiet corner for relaxation and pastoral conversations.[7]

Peppercorn Place, St Mary's, Marshalswick.

Even more useful than garden spaces are car parks. These are vital assets for churches with worshippers who drive to church. Car parks serve to increase accessibility to church on at least three grounds. First, they make available a guaranteed number of parking places to the church, so that worshippers do not have to compete with other users on the open road or in public car parks. Second, in busy urban areas, where parking is expensive, a church car park can represent a significant saving in the cost of coming to church; this in turn means the worshipper has more disposable income to donate to the ministry of the parish – a much better use of their money. Third, car parks on the site of a church itself can allow those with mobility issues to get close to the building, again increasing their likelihood to attend.

Around the week, church car parks assist the operational life of a church by providing on-site facilities for those coming for meetings, pastoral conversations, or work (e.g. staff and contractors). They are also a huge asset if they can be used by weekday hirers of the church or hall. Hirers may need to bring equipment on and off the site. If you can give them a guaranteed parking space, it greatly increases the attractiveness and value of your venue to them.

Some churches may be blessed with more parking spaces than they need, especially during the week. In some locations, this would represent a maintenance liability; in other settings, there may be money to be made from renting out these spaces.

- St Mary's, Rhossili, is in a remote rural location but near a popular walking destination. For many years, it ran a church car park with a simple honesty box. This has recently been replaced with a flat charge, perhaps due to the decline of cash.
- Holy Trinity, in the centre of Llandudno, has operated a commercial car park around the church for many years.

Churches are unlikely to want the hassle of administering a car park; but professional companies that are in the market can step into the gap. Some of these, such as JustPark, have experience of the opportunities and idiosyncrasies of working with churches.[8]

Further income will accrue to churches that can install electric-vehicle (EV) charging equipment in their car parks. If you are thinking about the possibilities of EV charging, you might like to consider:

- Your market. Do you envisage worshippers charging their cars during a service or hall hirers during a let? Or will there be more demand from local residents overnight? Getting a handle on this will influence the speed of charger you install. Overnight charging might be best served by a simple domestic charger that runs at 7.4 kW. Charging for a few hours during a visit to church or your hall would probably require a device that runs at more than 20 kW. Some very rapid chargers operate at considerably quicker speeds; but, unless you are planning to open a motorway service station, this is unlikely to be the device for you.
- Your demand. While it is good to incentivize green transport, you don't want to set aside parking bays for charging if they will be only infrequently used. It might be better to start out small and build up as the revolution in green transport gathers pace. You should engage an EV-charging company to find out how to get the best use out of the space available. Can you discourage general parking in an EV-charging spot by signage or laying coloured tarmac? Can you maximize potential earnings by nudging fully charged cars to promptly vacate by, for example, including an overstay fee on the charging app?
- Your power supply. Do you have enough electricity for the job? There is only a limited amount of power available from each local substation. The demand for electricity is only going to increase as we make the transition away from fossil fuels. So, if you think you may need more power, it is worth getting in early and bagging it from the supplier before someone else does.
- Your funding model. Assuming that there is sufficient electricity in the local grid, anyone can pay to have an EV-charger installed. However, your church may not have the cash available and it may seem like a bit of a gamble. Some EV-charger installers will fund an installation in return for a small annual fee, if you allow them to keep the profits from the envisaged charging. However, if a company is pushing a fully funded model, might that be an indication of decent levels of demand, the surplus of which you could retain if you were to stump up the initial installation costs?
- Your layout. Get the right site for your charger. The further it is from an existing supply of electricity, the more expensive it will be to install; and the more complicated it may be to get permission. Bear

in mind that the bulk of the installation cost will be for excavating the trench for, and laying, the wires, rather than for the charging unit itself. An ideal location to minimize the cabling work would be on an exterior wall of your church or hall. But this might not be possible for a whole host of reasons. The charger needs to be visible and easily accessible, including to drivers who use wheelchairs. Planning authorities are likely to prefer locations that are away from historic buildings and heritage walls. Finally, if your car park is liable to flooding, talk to your installation provider to make sure that the electrical equipment is contained in the head of the charger. Also, nothing should be exposed or vulnerable near the foot of the device.

Another enhancement that you might like to consider for your car park is a bike rack. These don't directly generate money like an EV-charger, but they are good for your green credentials. They may also free up car parking for those who really need it. Don't buy the evil V-shape wall-mounted stands because these are guaranteed to bend the wheels of any bikes wedged into them. Much better is a sturdy 'Sheffield toast rack', which can be procured for a few hundred pounds.

Car parks are not without their liabilities. They can be costly to maintain, especially if you need to renew the tarmac. They can be subject to many of the problems that churchyards have, especially as regards the condition of walls and the size of trees. They can create issues of management: how do you stop people abusing the space and parking for free if they are not coming to the church or hall? They can also disincentivize environmental best practice if they make it too easy to drive to church. None of these issues is beyond resolution, either through technical solutions or cultural nudges; in the long run, the cost of maintenance should work out to be less than the value of the car park as an asset, if the church has a reasonable footfall throughout the week.

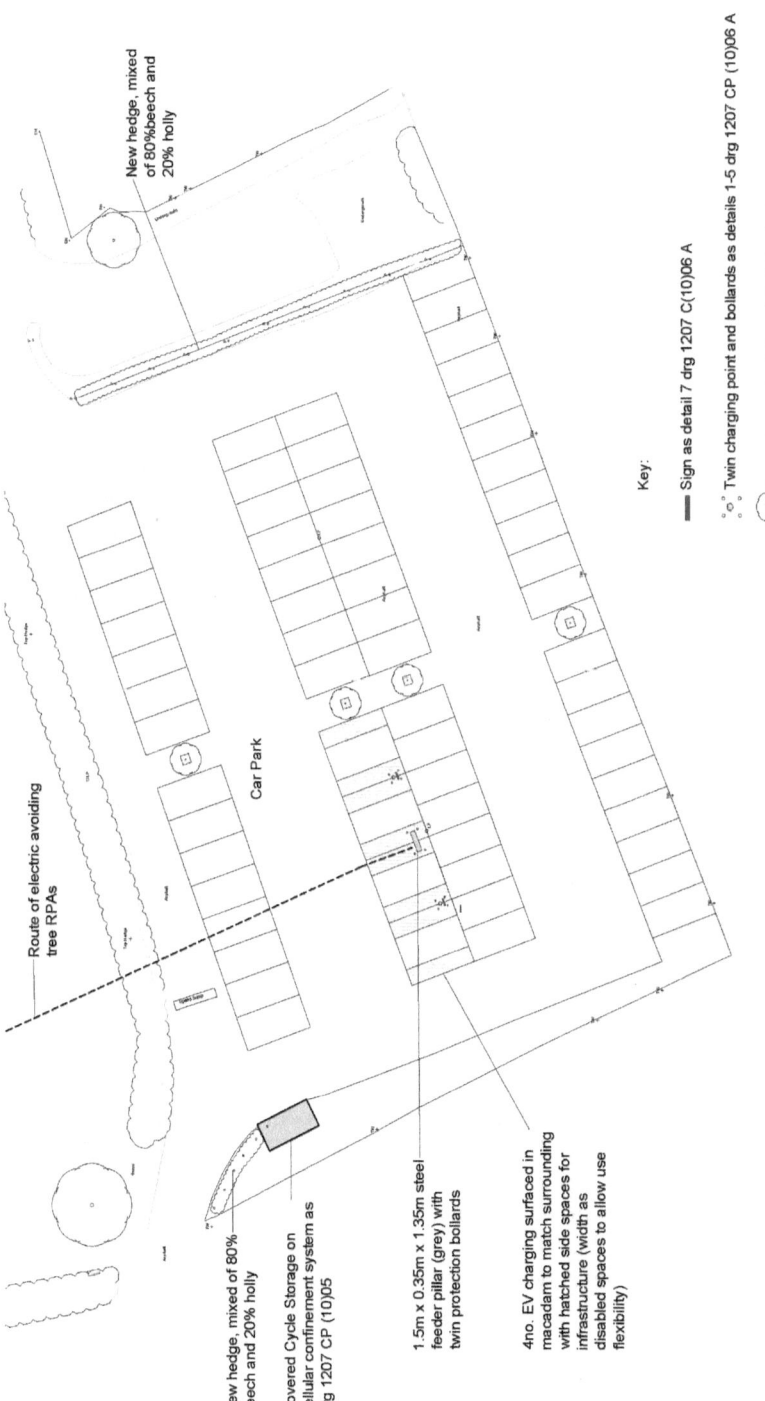

Electric-vehicle charging and bike rack proposals, *Salisbury Cathedral*, 2024.

Blessed plot

When that garden at St Mary's, Childwick Green, returned to parish management, I sat through endless meetings about how to make the best use of what looked like an ambiguous piece of land. But if I learned one thing from that process, it is that selling land (and other capital assets for that matter) should be avoided in almost all cases. We received offers for the land on several occasions; but we knew that these fell short of what we might achieve should we really want to sell. Moreover, even if the garden represented a present liability to the church, it would add immeasurably to the value of the site, should the church ever be sold for redevelopment as housing. This was not on the cards; but we rightly explored the issue from every angle. We concluded that a sale for conversion to housing would need a piece of land to facilitate a garage and garden. Finally, although we didn't know it at the time, it now strikes me that the garden at St Mary's represents an ideal appendage should the church ever wish to drill to allow a ground source heat-pump system.

This chapter began by lining up all the challenges that are created by land management for the local church. If you have a garden area, car park or – especially – a churchyard, worries and costs will surely follow. Nonetheless, the hands-on principles, reviewed in the earlier chapters about managing church buildings, apply equally to church land: almost always there are marginal improvements that can be made at relatively little cost; often, missional benefits can be wrought that would be impossible to quantify in purely monetary terms; and usually, over the long term, liabilities can be minimized and potential realized.

Notes

1 https://www.northwessexdowns.org.uk/wp-content/uploads/2021/11/Lighting_Guide_07-05_MEDRES.pdf (accessed 12.3.25).
2 https://www.plantlife.org.uk (accessed 12.3.25).
3 https://www.caringforgodsacre.org.uk (accessed 12.3.25).
4 e.g. https://www.churchofengland.org/resources/churchcare/advice-and-guidance-church-buildings/outdoor-worship (accessed 12.3.25).
5 https://engageworship.org/ideas/outdoor-worship-stations (accessed 12.3.25).
6 Thomas Gray, 1751, 'Elegy written in a country churchyard'.
7 https://www.marshalswick.org.uk/peppercornplace.htm (accessed 12.3.25).
8 https://stalbansdiocese.org/wp-content/uploads/2024/08/JustPark-Church-Car-Parks.pdf (accessed 12.3.25).

7

Making the most of your church hall

Among the many ambiguous legacies of the Victorian era is a sense that church buildings should be separate and sacred (Walter, 2011). A by-product of this legacy is the church hall. And, for some congregations, the prospect of having to manage a hall as well as a place of worship only adds to their headaches. The aim of this chapter is to reverse the chain of argument by uncovering the ways in which well-managed halls can benefit the mission of local Christian communities.

The nineteenth century ushered in a period of dramatic renovation of churches and the construction of new ones. Many of these projects were inspired by the principles of the Anglo-Catholic revival within the Church of England. The emphasis of this movement, on the worship of God in the beauty of holiness, led to magnificent buildings that were intended exclusively for liturgy. Churches were laid out with elaborate sanctuaries and lots of fixed furniture, such as pews and organs. Communities up and down the land continue to enjoy these wonderful spaces. However, they have a flip side. By using churches only for worship, other functions that might once have been conducted in the nave or vestry or church porch were forced into alternative venues. As a result, alongside their new and renovated churches, the Victorians also built halls. These were intended as more secular spaces in which communities could meet for social, educational and welfare purposes. Churches have continued this tradition until quite recently, complementing relatively inflexible worship spaces with multi-purpose halls that can be used by the whole community throughout the week. Not every church has a hall of course, especially in smaller communities and rural areas. In these instances, multi-purpose use of the church is more likely to have been retained or restored.

SWOT

Church halls come in different shapes and sizes. Some are very small, others are cavernous barns. Some are free-standing, either on the same site as the church or at a different location nearby. Quite a few are actually attached to the place of worship, either integral to the whole or accessed via an adjoining corridor. St Barnabas', Dulwich, has examples of all three types of hall:[1]

- St Barnabas' Parish Hall is a free-standing building, a quarter of a mile from the church;
- the Community Suite is a part of the worship space that can be compartmentalized from the nave of the church;
- the Lounge is an earlier part of the site linked to the church by a corridor.

Inevitably, such diverse facilities are equipped in different ways, for different purposes, and attract widely differing uses through the week and across the year.

Additional buildings run the risk of creating extra worries for those charged with care and maintenance. Furthermore, halls are attended by their own unique problems. Historically, not all halls were built to the same standards as the church. Often, they were constructed after the church and on slimmer budgets. They can be impaired by poor foundations, thin walls, cheap roofs, and so on. Frequently, they have not been maintained as well as the adjacent church: when the pennies are tight, congregations understandably devote attention and resources to the worship space first. Finally, because many halls have a heavy footfall, any slippage of maintenance can soon lead to deterioration in the condition of the building.

However, just as I believe churches can be turned from millstones into mission tools, the same is true of church halls. Halls offer opportunities for direct outreach into the community. For example, people who attend an exercise group in the hall may feel more comfortable to call into the adjacent church immediately before or after their group. Or they may feel a sufficient connection to return for a service at Christmas or Easter. Hall users are also likely to come into contact with the regular congregation, through which friendships may develop. And church halls act as giant free noticeboards: platforms for publicity through posters, electronic screens and leaflets. Appropriate parish marketing can be targeted at known users of a hall: for example, families.

It is also possible to make direct approaches to hirers of your church hall and so build working relationships. Some uniformed organizations, such as, Scouts and Guides, may be open to occasional input from the vicar or other licensed minister. Not all groups welcome such advances of course, so each conversation needs to be handled with respect. Another direct approach might be to ask members of a hall-hire group to get involved in the church's worship at an appropriate time of the year, either thematically (such as Young Farmers at Harvest) or generically (such as sharing out readings for the Christmas carol service to representatives of your hall-hire groups). Some will probably say no; for others, it might be just the opening for which they have been waiting.

Moreover, if halls are well managed and maintained, they can become a significant source of additional income that a church can then plough back into its ministry and other projects. Churches should 'sweat their assets' (to adopt a ghastly phrase) and, in many cases, the hall will be the sweatiest thing they possess. Indeed, the PCC (or equivalent trustees) are under a legal obligation to seek market return on their assets – an important principle to which we will return shortly. Despite this, the usefulness of halls to the mission and finance of local congregations has often been ignored. This is because the prevailing argument of much training about parish finance emphasizes the importance of congregational giving campaigns, sometimes to the detriment of other valuable income streams. I have attended several training events about giving campaigns; the argument is that congregational donations are the largest source of income for most churches, therefore churches should target this committed core for increased future funding. I have never accepted this logic. In an age when many churches face rising costs, it is invidious to turn inward to those who have given so generously in the past. This is especially true when congregations are elderly: many will be on fixed pensions, while the parish share request from the diocese often rises at a rate that represents a real terms increase for each worshipper. Undoubtedly congregational support will remain the most significant income line on most churches' accounts; but regular supporters will be more confident about giving generously if they know that their generosity is buttressed by other means. A mix of income sources is much more robust than a monoculture of congregational giving. Thus halls have a vital contribution to play for churches that are seeking a portfolio of diversified income.

Good management of halls covers a plethora of issues around finance and marketing, maintenance and development. In addition to all of these – indeed as a matter of prior consideration – churches need to affirm where their halls fit into their mission strategy. Let's explore these issues through the lens of a worked example: the halls that I know best from my time as Vicar of St Michael's with St Mary's in St Albans, as well as other halls run by neighbouring churches within St Albans deanery.

Worked example: church halls in St Albans

Starting point

There is an old adage which says that if you are looking to get to a certain destination, it would be better to start from somewhere else. However, in reality, we can only ever start from where we find ourselves. Given this, when I arrived to be Vicar of St Michael's with St Mary's in 2012, I was keen to get an early handle not only on the church buildings but also on the halls for which the parish was responsible. There are three of these and they are completely different in size, location, age, condition, purpose and potential.

Closest to home was the Parish Centre. I could see this from the windows of the vicarage, standing in the adjacent churchyard at St Michael's. The Parish Centre had been built in the 1970s to replace a small Victorian schoolroom, which had, itself, stood on the site of the town's former workhouse. The Parish Centre is a two-storey building that had a kitchen, a small hall downstairs, and a larger hall upstairs, with an accessible toilet. It was well built and subsequently well maintained by an active congregation. I was informed on arrival that it was used for a range of meetings and children's parties throughout the week, in addition to our busy programme of church activities. It was professionally managed by the Parish Administrator; it generated over £20,000 a year: more than enough to cover its costs. So far so good.

Out of town, in the hamlet of Childwickbury, St Mary's Church was adjoined, through a corridor, by a parallel hall. Here is an example of the classic Victorian parish room. It even retained its original title of 'Schoolroom'; it had been built to facilitate rudimentary education for the children of workers on the Childwickbury estate. This function had ceased in the 1920s; a small amount of congregational use, mainly social, had continued in its wake. During the week, a couple of art groups met; these generated a few thousand pounds a year. Monies were usually paid in cash, sometimes left in little envelopes on windowsills or beside the kettle in the kitchenette, which had been craftily inserted into the corridor between the church and Schoolroom. It was blindingly obvious that the contents of these envelopes were not going to cover the liabilities of the building. The Schoolroom itself was tired and deteriorating: windows were damaged; the lighting was on its last legs; the décor was poor. There was an alarming crack opening in the east wall. And the floor was collapsing from rot in all four corners. A faint mustiness hung in the air. The overall impression was complemented outside by a dangerous lean-to on the east of the kitchenette corridor, which covered a subterranean disused boiler house, a freezing-cold freestanding toilet around the back, and a small car park that turned to mud at the first sight of winter rain.

But there was more to come: the Memorial Hall on Branch Road. This large brick edifice with toilets, kitchen, a small meeting room and extensive storage, had been raised to commemorate the 65 men of the parish who had given their lives during the First World War. It stands on a suburban street, about half a mile from St Michael's Church. The parish profile, at the time of my appointment, said that the Memorial Hall does not belong to the church but that 'the Stewardship Committee of the PCC has a watching brief over its maintenance'. Err, no. Within days of my arrival, it became patently clear that the PCC was entirely responsible for the hall, holding it on a long lease from a significant local landowner. The hall had been partially forgotten by the parish, I suspect because most of the churchy needs had been met since the 1970s by the Parish Centre at St Michael's. The end result was that the Memorial Hall had been cared for faithfully by one parishioner, a dedicated and godly steward. But they had many family and work commitments, and lacked the time and budget to staunch the wounds of a gradually decaying building. Fortunately, the hall was largely proofed against the elements, although the single glazing was starting to leak. Inside, the internal paintwork looked dreadful and the flooring was lifting. The dilapidated kitchen was a bio-hazard waiting to infect its hirers. Outside, the grounds were overgrown and attracted antisocial behaviour. The main user of the hall was a nursery school; there were also a handful of sports groups that met during the evenings. This included an archery group the arrows of which had been known to pierce the east door of the building: the last barrier between the bowmen and innocent pedestrians outside. Unsurprisingly, given the condition of the hall, all the hirers were on ridiculously cheap rates, collectively generating about £14,000 a year. It was clear that things needed to be done – and quickly. Things were not good at St Mary's – we will return to the Schoolroom shortly – but paramount attention had to be given to the Memorial Hall if the parish were not to receive a visit from the local building control or the Health and Safety Executive.

Building plan

On coming into the parish as a new vicar, my first priority was to support the hard-working volunteer who oversaw the Memorial Hall. Fortunately, it was not too difficult to persuade a number of people to join a small committee to plan for the future of this hall. I was careful not to ask any of the hirers themselves because I feared we would soon run into intractable conflicts of interest. However, there was a groundswell of support from those who lived nearby and who used the services of the nursery. Two young mums proved especially helpful. They brought energy, vision and time. Together we could begin to work on the condition of the building and how it was run.

The committee began to get a handle on the situation by commissioning a condition survey of the hall. We paid our church architect to write a report on the state of the building and to make recommendations about what should be done to improve it. Unlike Anglican churches, which are subject to compulsory quinquennial inspections (QIs), the same rule does not apply to halls if they are freestanding from the church. Nonetheless, condition surveys are an invaluable starting point; I cannot recommend them enough. They are a relatively inexpensive and objective means of getting a baseline assessment of the state of a building, and what needs doing to it. If you're lucky, or request it, the architect will also throw in some ballpark costings.

One of the most pressing issues identified by the condition survey of the Memorial Hall was that the main window at the gable end was well past its sell-by date. Either the victim of vandals without or those archers within, some of the glass quarries had come out of the leading, while others were cracked. This was not just a heating problem and a safety issue. It was, literally, our shop window: it faced the main road that ran past the hall. The old window looked tired and uninviting, especially to potential hirers. It was evident that a replacement window would give an immediate facelift to the whole operation.

An uninviting frontage before refurbishment: overgrown trees, a broken window, tired paintwork, an arrow-riddled door, and a tatty noticeboard at St Michael's Memorial Hall.

Need was met by resource in the form of a small grant from our county councillor. A chance conversation with the councillor netted us a 'locality' grant. This £500 was exactly the right sum to replace the old window with a decent double-glazed upgrade. It proved to be amazing seedcorn because it demonstrated to the hall committee the impact of carefully directed interventions in the building. It was just what we needed to kickstart a rolling programme of repairs and improvements.

More than ten years later, that £500 grant has mushroomed into an investment of £100,000 of targeted expenditure. No longer on the back foot, the Memorial Hall is now an attractive and functional meeting space. Asbestos has been identified and removed or made safe. The bubbling lino on the floor has been replaced. The heating system has been improved, with a more efficient boiler and extra lagging on the pipes. The awful kitchen that was once filled with repurposed domestic units has been replaced; it is now an appropriately equipped and hygienic space. Old strip-lights and high-consumption halogens have been replaced with environmentally friendly LEDs that better illuminate the features of the building. The windows throughout have been upgraded to double-glazing, driving an immediate 30 per cent reduction in heating bills. A full schedule of testing has been instituted and remedial actions undertaken (gas, fire extinguishers, fire detection and evacuation, electrical wiring, portable appliances, and so on). Exploratory consideration has been given to possibly placing solar panels on the south-facing roof. Inside, the building has had a good clean and clutter has been removed. Outside, the grounds have been pared back to remove the discarded condoms and drugs paraphernalia.

Professional admin

None of these improvements to the building would have been possible without a corresponding step-change in the way that the Memorial Hall was run. As so often, these developments occur as a result of happenstance as much as deliberate planning. But looking back, they somehow all fit together.

A year or two after my appointment as the vicar, I was visited by the two mums whom I had persuaded to join the Memorial Hall committee.

'We've been thinking,' began Rosie and Danielle.

'*Oh dear*,' I thought, as I straightened myself in my chair and braced for whatever suggestion was about to be unleashed on an unsuspecting world.

'What the Memorial Hall really needs is a professional administrator.'

Rosie and Danielle started to outline their case about what this post would contribute to the efficient organization of hirers and to the collection of income. I was really impressed. They made a convincing argument, including a business case about the potential for future growth. The part-time post would, as a result, become self-financing.

'Great,' I said. 'Let me propose it to the PCC.'

'Excellent,' they replied. 'And, by the way, Danielle is looking for a job.'

The appointment of Danielle as administrator of the Memorial Hall proved an unqualified success. Temperamentally, she was well suited to the role, combining good interpersonal skills with steely determination. She was also open to change and committed to finding better ways of doing things. Her appointment soon identified a raft of good practice that was needed. Some of this Danielle adapted from systems at the Parish Centre, which was already professionally run by another colleague. But some of this had to be shaped specifically for the Memorial Hall. It would take Danielle several years of dogged determination to change the systemic culture of the parish towards this hall, as well as the attitudes that had built up among the hirers. She oversaw all this with persistence and good humour.

Ts & Cs

First, Danielle needed to present the hirers of the Memorial Hall with proper terms and conditions. Most of these could be adapted from the documentation used at the Parish Centre. Over the years, these terms have evolved further in response to needs that have been identified.

Terms and conditions are crucial to building good relations with hirers. This is because they set out clear mutual obligations and expectations. If your hall does not have any terms and conditions and you are starting from scratch, it is probably worth cribbing them from another church or seeking input from your diocese. St Michael's terms and conditions are available.[2] The redoubtable John Truscott, a church consultant and trainer, also has some useful templates on his website.[3]

Particular consideration should be given, in terms and conditions, to a number of issues. If necessary, further conversation with the hirer might be needed to ensure that everyone is on the same page.

- Safeguarding. This is paramount. Depending on what the hirer wants to do in the building, they may need their own safeguarding policy and procedures – and to provide evidence of this. Groups that are not working with children or vulnerable adults may be able to adopt

the policy of your parish. Advice should be sought from the parish or diocesan safeguarding officers about best practice in this area.
- Access. How will the hirer get into the building and when? Can they enter the whole site or are parts of the building being used by someone else or off limits for other reasons: e.g. safeguarding? Has enough time been allowed for setting up and taking down?

    When I arrived in the parish, all three halls were accessed by means of a key, which each hirer had to collect from a keyholder. This system was fraught with difficulties. Hirers had to walk several hundred yards between the hall and the keyholder at the start and end of each session. The hiring schedule meant that keyholders felt tied down for large swathes of the day. And each keyholder represented a potential single point of failure, especially since one of them was nearly ninety. To get around these problems, we installed coded locks on the doors of each hall. The Memorial Hall and Parish Centre had electronic devices fitted; these enabled Danielle to give different codes to different hirers and to cancel them if a hirer left us, or if we suspected the number was becoming too well known. In the case of the Parish Centre, the lock also had a timer so that the access number only worked when the hirer was permitted to use the building; this was an important requirement because of the confidentiality and safeguarding requirements of some of the hirers. Footfall at the Schoolroom was less pressured, so a manual push-button lock proved to be sufficient there.
- Alcohol. Unless a hall has a licensed bar, there will be limited times in the year when booze can be sold on the premises. Sales of alcoholic drinks are permitted via a temporary event notice (TEN) issued by the local authority. We required hirers to apply for TENs if they wished to sell alcohol. However, because the TENs limit accrues to the venue, not the hirer, Danielle rightly insisted that hirers liaised with her in advance, so that we did not exceed the number of TENs we were allowed each year. Also, the church might need a TEN should we want to sell drinks at a parish event.
- Insurance. Your hall will need to be insured. The Ecclesiastical Insurance Group (EIG), which covers most Church of England churches, also offers tailor-made insurance for halls. And it can provide churches and halls together with a single, discounted parish package. In addition, EIG is very good at advising about ways in

which risks can be reduced. Insurance is also required of regular groups who hire a hall. Public liability cover is a particular consideration here. You should decide whether to ask hirers to submit a copy of their insurance at the time of booking or on an annual basis, if they are regulars.
- Deposits. These can be a prudent means of securing a booking so that a hirer does not let you down by cancelling at the last minute, leaving a gap in the diary. Deposits can also be taken against damage done during the booking, which may in turn ensure that hirers remain on their best behaviour. That said, the administration of deposits brings inevitable hassle, which should be weighed against the added security that they offer.
- Internet. If the hall has wifi, what are the terms under which you will permit the Internet to be accessed? Are the settings on the wifi secure? Does the church wish to block certain types of activity on its wifi?
- Music and video streaming. With or without wifi, hirers may want to play music or videos during their use of your hall. Licences are available through Christian Copyright Licensing International[4] and the Performing Right Society.[5] Both these bodies can also provide advice about what are sometimes complex matters of permission and copyright.
- Storage. This is always a hoary issue. Regular hirers often want cupboard space or other storage in which to keep their equipment between sessions. Most halls do not have sufficient capacity. Clarity should be established before a hire begins about what, if anything, is available. If storage is permitted, advice may need to be sought as regards who takes responsibility for contents insurance.
- Risks and training. Regular hirers will need their own risk assessments for what they are doing in your building. Depending on the nature of their activity, they may also need to have undertaken training, e.g. in food hygiene or first aid. Does the church need to see evidence that the hirers have such procedures in place? Alternatively, is it sufficient to have advised hirers about their responsibilities in this regard?

As Danielle got to grips with her administrative tasks, a couple of knotty legal problems were uncovered. As a memorial to victims of the First

World War, the hall and its land was on a 99-year lease from a local landholder. The lease was due to lapse in the mid 2020s, so the parish entered negotiations to extend the lease in order to be able to invest with confidence in our intended improvements to the hall. We were delighted that the landholder appreciated the value of the hall to the community and was willing to extend our lease. This superior lease conveyed responsibilities on the PCC: for example, to notify the landowner about certain works that were proposed on the building and about the nature of our relationship with the major user of the building, the nursery school.

This last point was important because we were advised that the occupation of the building by the nursery was of a magnitude that required it to be subject not to simple terms and conditions, but to a sublease drawn up by a solicitor. This in turn was paired with another legal document: a licence to cover permanent storage facilities that the nursery had on site.

The PCC was supported in these legal processes by the diocese, which was itself a party to the leases. This is because, in the Church of England system, the PCC is the 'managing trustee' of the assets of a parish but the Diocesan Board of Finance acts as the backstop 'custodian trustee'. Undertaking this legal work was not cheap, but we were grateful eventually to iron out the issues. We were aware of a nearby church that was getting into hot water because of a similar historic arrangement with a pre-school. In its case, the rights and responsibilities were not clearly agreed and documented. Do seek advice from your diocese or other legal expert if in doubt about this area.

While considering these legalities, you should also keep an eye on your liability for business rates. Rates are assessed by the government's Valuation Office Agency[6] and are payable to the local authority. The system is labyrinthine but, in summary, rates may be payable, depending on how your hall is being used.

Business plan

Not only did Danielle roll-out detailed terms and conditions for the hirers, she was also instrumental in making the Memorial Hall pay its way. We knew that the hall had to increase its income. About £20,000 p.a. was needed to break-even on routine maintenance, cleaning and utilities. More would be necessary if we were going to make long-term improvements. In the space of three short years, Danielle took the income of the hall from £14,000 to £40,000. This was a staggering achievement. This meant, in the long run, that once the backlog of maintenance had been cleared, the Memorial Hall had the potential to plough a significant surplus into parish funds every year: a big sum for a parish like St Michael's.

How was Danielle able to increase revenue so much? In short, she attracted more groups and got them to pay more money. One of the early actions taken by the PCC, as regards all three halls, was to seek reassurance that we were charging appropriate rates. While it might have been possible to phone around other churches and hall operators in the area and ask them their prices, this would have only provided a crude assessment of the market. We chose instead to pay an independent quantity surveyor (QS), sourced through the diocese, to undertake the research for us. For a very modest fee, he visited all three halls, assessed their condition, location and potential uses, and recommended the market rates for regular and one-off hirers. His report also commented on the overall condition of the halls; he made suggestions about improvements we could make if we were seeking to raise the charges.

The results of the rate review were revelatory. It showed that charges at the Parish Centre were set at about the right level: it wouldn't be appropriate to push things there. However, the feedback indicated that we were charging well below market rate for St Mary's Schoolroom and the Memorial Hall. In one instance, a sports group in the Memorial Hall was deemed to be paying just one third of the recommended market rate.

Having read the review, the PCC agreed that charges would have to increase. Danielle embraced this challenge with enthusiasm. Letters were carefully drafted to all the hirers to advise them about where they sat in relation to the independent review. Where there was a big gap between what they were paying and what they should be paying, individual meetings were convened and negotiations opened. Why the rates needed to go up and the dates by which we expected the new rate to be achieved were discussed. This had to be done with sensitivity. Tapered arrangements were established for some groups. Doing so allowed them to meet the increase over a number of months, so that the new rate did not come as an immediate shock to the groups' treasurers or members.

Inevitably there was some disquiet. One group insisted on retaining their old rate. We feared they might go to the media, so a carefully worded pre-emptive press-release was prepared. In the end, nothing came of it, in part, I suspect, because the parish's position was watertight. Two things came to our aid. First, conducting a rate review through an independent QS left the complainants without room for manoeuvre. The parish could double down on the argument that our new prices had been objectively benchmarked; and, if a group really thought it could do better elsewhere, it was welcome to check out the competition. Few did. Even fewer left. The second pillar on which the parish could lean was the Charities Act. Under the terms of this legislation, trustees have a duty to seek a market return on assets. Were the PCC not to charge market rate to hall hirers, it would effectively be subsidizing the hirers' activities from other funds – of which the largest proportion came from regular, faithful giving by the congregation. And this would be perverse: worshippers give to their church to sustain ministry and their place of worship, not to subsidize indirectly the local badminton club on a Tuesday evening.

This argument proved irrefutable: most groups saw the fairness of the new arrangement and came on board. Those that left merely freed up slots for others who were ready and willing to hire the hall at the market rate. The cost of the survey was rapidly covered by increased income. The process was so successful that we undertook to repeat the exercise every three years. This meant that rates never slipped behind the market level. Confidence could also be built among our hirers because they knew that their rate would be fixed for three years, and then they could expect a review.

Two exceptions might be made to the above charging policy. First, when a group's activities align with those of the parish, it might reasonably attract a discount. Discount here does not mean subsidy: the church can still charge a rate that covers the costs of having the group in the building, while acknowledging the worthiness of the group's activities by offering a reduced hire fee. An initial discount might be offered to all charities because they are not seeking to turn a profit. Further discounts might apply to groups with activities that are closely allied with the goals of the church's Mission Action Plan (MAP) or an equivalent strategy. (Obvious examples here might be the pastoral care offered to the vulnerable through an Alcoholics Anonymous meeting, or to those supporting local families through uniformed organizations.)

Conversely, there may be some groups undertaking activities considered antipathetic or even antagonistic to the goals of the church. Certain political activity might fall into this category. Some Christians are cautious about physical exercise disciplines that originate in other religious traditions. It would be unreasonable to charge higher rates for such activities – that would be profiteering – but there might be circumstances under which a group is not permitted use of the building. Caution is needed here. A church leadership will be keen to uphold their integrity; however, they should consider whether barring a group might be discriminatory – or perceived to be discriminatory – and so cause reputational damage. Conversely, might failure to block a radical group facilitate extremism? Legal advice may be needed. In general, in the interests of welcome and free debate, I personally favour keeping the door as open as possible.

Business and building plans in tandem

The revival of the fortunes of the Memorial Hall was the cumulative effect of a number of actions. These were not necessarily all planned meticulously in advance: some were reactions to pressing needs. Sometimes, however, a less evolutionary and more deliberative plan is needed: a context that requires an integrated proposal for the care of the building, with a realistic business model. A few years into my time as the vicar, I realized that this would be necessary if we were to rescue the Schoolroom at St Mary's, Childwick Green, from desuetude. A significant uplift would be needed in the fabric of the hall if it were to draw in the new people who might secure its long-term flourishing. As so often, God presented an opening for this change and, in due course, the funds to undertake it.

The year 2017 was a big one for little St Mary's. It was the church's 150th anniversary. The small committee that oversaw the management of the church naturally wanted to commemorate the milestone. This desire coincided with a review by the PCC of the MAP of the whole parish. Within this review, St Mary's discerned that they needed to be more open. This meant being more open at the front door to visitors (see p. 61 for the electronic door opening device). And it meant being more open at the back door to those who wanted to use the Schoolroom. The big problem was the overall state of the hall. Repairs in previous years had resolved some of the problems – the rotting floor, the old lighting and the tired décor. However, the worrying crack in the east wall was only growing bigger; we were also still plagued by the horrible outside toilet.

Reflecting on this need, the St Mary's committee agreed to explore constructing an internal toilet as a 150th anniversary project. We discerned that a good location would be on the east side of the corridor that linked the church and hall. The new toilet would fill in the unattractive and dangerous former boiler house and facilitate a simultaneous underpinning of the east wall of the Schoolroom. The position was also ideal in relation to the church and the hall because it would provide a facility that could be used by people without their necessarily interrupting the activities in either space.

It was a bold move. I was impressed by the committee's ambition. But I was also frightened by the implications. For a small church such as St Mary's, this project would represent the largest single investment on the site since the church had been built in 1867. The project would have to be constructed to a high standard commensurate with the Grade II listing of the church. And it would have to be built to the latest standards of accessibility, to ensure that it could be used by someone in a wheelchair. Sustainability was also a factor, to guarantee a low-carbon footprint. All this would mean money. And money was something that St Mary's did not have. The congregation had responded well when they had been confronted with the realistic costs of maintaining ministry in the church; they had increased their regular giving accordingly. And there was an endowment that generated a thousand or two every year for routine repairs and maintenance. But the ballpark estimate from our architect for the toilet scheme was £100,000. It seemed a huge mountain to have to climb.

Faced with such a challenge, we needed to look hard at where the money might come from before we could commission a scheme. Several potential streams emerged. First Danielle, our Halls Administrator, produced a business case for the project. She based this on the increased income that she anticipated might reasonably accrue from the Schoolroom, should a toilet be installed. Without an internal loo, she found it very hard to promote the room to any hirers. With a loo, it would become an interesting proposition for anyone wanting an attractive

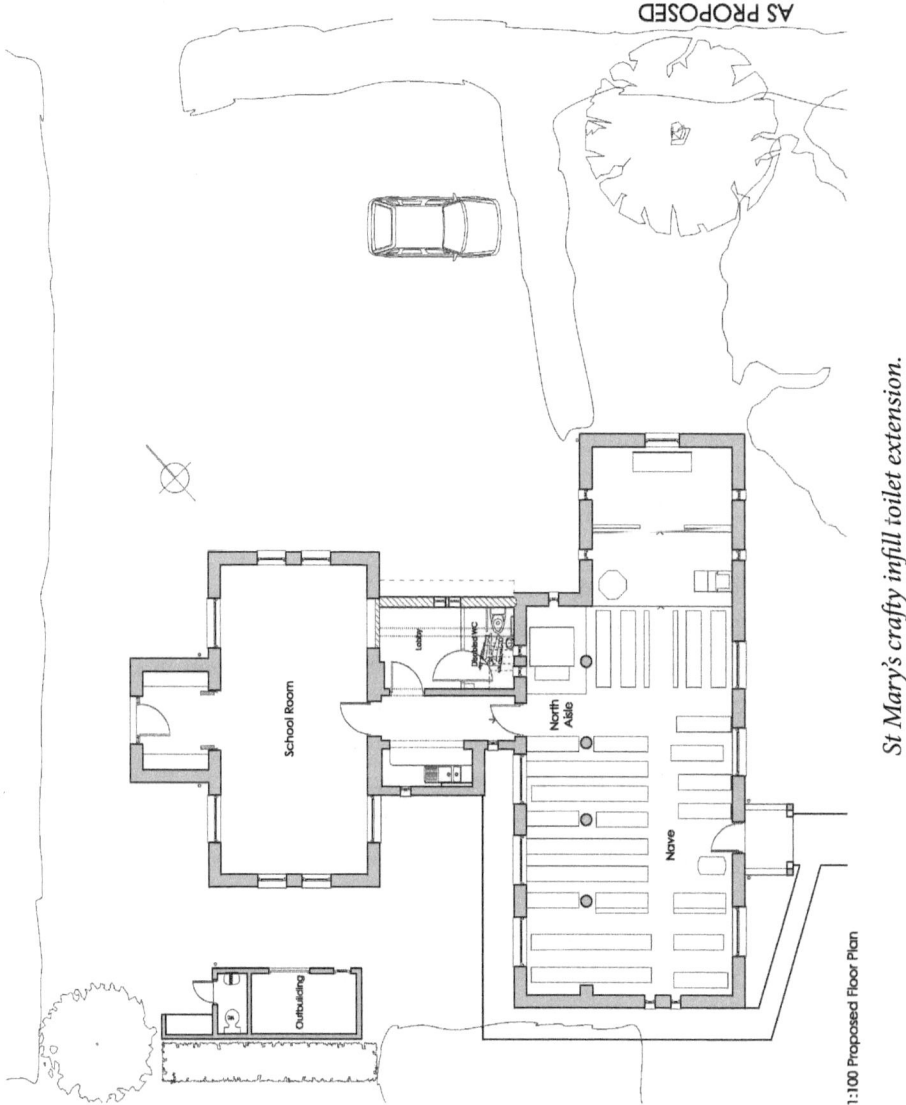

St Mary's crafty infill toilet extension.

AS PROPOSED

1:100 Proposed Floor Plan

heritage venue, in a beautiful rural location, conveniently accessible from St Albans and Harpenden. Danielle projected that, after three years, she might reasonably take the hall from its income of less than £4,000 p.a. to more than £10,000 p.a.

This projection gave me confidence to lay the whole project before the PCC. The PCC was responsible for both churches, but the vast majority of the reserves belonged to the larger St Michael's. Could St Michael's be persuaded to underwrite the toilet project at its sister church in return for repayment from the increased letting of the Schoolroom? I pitched for a loan from St Michael's to St Mary's of £50,000, repayable over ten years. It was a big ask and I wasn't sure how it was going to land. To my complete surprise, the parish treasurer (so often and so rightly the voice of caution) argued at the PCC meeting that St Michael's should not lend the sum to St Mary's. Rather, she said, St Michael's should give St Mary's the money. The treasurer's rationale was that a gift would enable St Mary's to seek the funding to be matched with confidence from grants and private donors, and not to be burdened with worries about repayment. Also – the treasurer had not abandoned prudence either – she argued that drawing in such outside funds to achieve the toilet extension would increase the capital value of the PCC's asset at St Mary's. I was arrested by the clarity of this thinking. I was even more bowled over when the PCC unanimously approved the treasurer's amendment. A representative of St Mary's, often reserved in demeanour, was moved to tears by this act of generosity.

Having secured half the funds from the PCC, the next challenge was to find the remainder. This would mean bids to individuals and grant-making bodies. St Mary's committee could think of a few charities to which we might apply but it all seemed a bit nebulous. At this point the diocese came to our rescue in the form of the Historic Church Buildings Support Officer. This officer was not going to make the grant applications for us; he did, however, maintain lists of charities to which a parish might turn, depending on the nature of its project. Armed with the Buildings Support Officer's 'kitchens and loos' list, we identified about ten charities to which we might have a fighting chance of pitching our project. Inevitably, we had to craft an individual application to each. Some wanted a covering letter. Others had complicated forms. One organization had an interminable online document, with three discrete hurdles to clear before they told us whether we would get any dosh.

None asked exactly the same questions. None had identical objectives. We would need to persevere and adapt our project so as to attract the attention of each. Of the ten grant-making bodies that we approached, we were delighted to receive grants from five. The biggest of these was from the body with that deadly online form and multiple gateways: Veolia Environmental Trust. We almost gave up on their application because of all the information that they were requesting. Even when we had cleared the final application round, I thought they might, at best, give us £10,000. They came up trumps and put in £27,000.

Hot on the heels of the grant-making bodies came personal gifts. We held an open afternoon and barbecue to promote the scheme to neighbours of the church, interested parties in the area, as well worshippers at both St Mary's and St Michael's. Several cheques were received as a result, including from people who had caught the vision but who had not been supporters of the church before.

The final strand of our fundraising campaign was to try to establish a friends' group for St Mary's. (For further advice and caution about friends' groups, see Walter and Mottram, pp. 265–99.) Although quite a lot of planning was put into the Friends of St Mary's initiative, the idea struggled to get traction and has since ceased. It was worth a try.

Fortunately, we did not need a friends' group to reach our target. Indeed, we were so successful with the gifts and grants that the final demand on the parish was considerably less than the £50,000 underwriting that they had agreed.

With funding secured, a tender process completed, and a minor skirmish fought with the local planning authority about the details of a window design, work started on site in the autumn of 2019. Construction was completed in early 2020 and the archdeacon was invited for a ceremonial first flush. It had taken several years of hard slog but the project was finally completed, on budget if not on time.

As it turned out, timing was immaterial, because we opened the new loo just weeks before the coronavirus shutdown. This meant that St Mary's could not immediately reap any of the benefits of the investment. However, as government restrictions on movement and gathering were lifted, St Mary's bounced back strongly. New hirers were attracted to the Schoolroom and new people joined the congregation – exactly as we had hoped. A church that once had liabilities greater than its income has been secured, for the long term, through a targeted building intervention and reasoned business case: a beacon of the gospel in a small hamlet.

The Forth Bridge principle

There are two final lessons that I learned from a decade of work with parish halls. The first is a reminder of the continuous nature of the task. Halls, like churches, are akin to the infamous Forth Bridge. Just as soon as one project or set of repairs have been completed, it is time to move on to the next. There is always more work to be done. I say this not as a counsel of despair nor a recipe for burnout, but as further reason for churches to get their halls into a good state of repair and management so that they can be operated on the front foot.

It is not just buildings that need continual refreshing. The same is also true of our people. Towards the end of my time in the parish, it became clear that new leadership was needed at the Memorial Hall. As a vicar, I was always keen to draw in new skills and energy and, with good grace and hearty thanks, to allow others to step back when requested. The parishioner who had worked so long and hard to oversee the Memorial Hall during its most difficult years chose to lay down the role. However, we were fortunate to draw in three younger dads in his place. Each brought different professional skills and community contacts, so when I left the parish in 2022, I knew that the maintenance of the hall remained in excellent hands.

Meanwhile, over at the parish office, it had been interesting to see the development of an online halls diary, so that prospective customers could view when slots were available in all three buildings. In addition, a full audit trail had been established through electronic booking forms, invoices, BACS payments and receipts. The days of cash-filled soggy envelopes were long gone.

The Internet has also beckoned an age of almost endless marketing possibilities, with 360-degree photographic tours, layout plans, technical specifications, and so on. Apps, such as sharesy.com, are revolutionizing how venues can promote their spaces to a wider audience. A similar platform, find-mushroom.com, has a focus on music rehearsal spaces, which could be relevant for many churches, as well as suitably equipped halls. Inevitably, such service providers charge for the privilege so, if you are going down this route, it would be worth comparing companies to make sure you have the right fee structure for your needs.

The second postscript to my learning about the contribution of halls to parish mission is the way in which we saw our breakthroughs encouraging others. Just as we had pinched best practice from colleagues – particular thanks to Matthew Stone and the communities of St John the Evangelist, Great Stanmore – so others started to borrow ideas from us.

Much of this came with recovery from the coronavirus restrictions in 2021. It was a time when churches and community organizations desperately needed to reconnect with people in three dimensions. It was also a time of uncertainty about future patterns of employment. Would employees continue to work flexibly from home? Would commuters be going back to offices in London, as they had before the pandemic? What was going to happen to those who had lost their jobs? Would they be looking for new opportunities, including establishing new businesses?

While grappling with questions like these, my colleagues in the deanery began a conversation that faced in two directions. The first was to speak with officers and elected members of the city council; they asked whether our church halls might support new entrepreneurial and social activity within the city. The council was being approached by individuals looking for cheap venues for start-ups and hot-desking space. At the same time, churches were hoping to attract new hirers. Following several meetings, we arranged for a database of all the church halls to be created. This included location, capacity, facilities, access, and so on, as well as indicative rates of hire, web links and contacts. This simple comparison tool was then mounted on the city council website as a means of funnelling the enquiries received at their offices.

Alongside this detailed but useful piece of comparative work, I arranged for Danielle to lead a workshop for parishes in the deanery who wished to gather and discuss halls management. Some had worries to share. Others were looking for fresh ideas. Danielle did an excellent presentation about what she had overseen and overcome at St Michael's and St Mary's, while empathizing that the contexts of every other parish would have their own unique challenges and solutions.

It was clear during the workshop that most of the church halls in the deanery were administered by unpaid worshippers, some of whom were near – or beyond – the point where they wanted to stop. It struck me that these churches probably needed to take the risk that we had and make a conscious effort to professionalize their halls administration. I also thought there could be considerable benefit if churches worked together in a syndicate to achieve this. No church would have a hall that could support a full-time halls administrator, but several parishes might collate their halls administration into a significant portfolio of work. Furthermore, the advantages of several parishes sharing a halls administrator would be that bookings could be maximized; if one hall could not accommodate an enquirer, the administrator would have access to the diaries of other local church venues that might.

In summary, parish halls administered well can offer a vital adjunct to churches' work within their localities. The more flexible you can make your hall, the wider the market you will reach. That's not to say that every hall will suit every potential hirer. Size, setting, style and fittings all influence the sort of hirers you are likely to attract. This is why networks of hall administration (or at least shared advertising) could allow a deanery or other consortium of churches to have the greatest market impact. And it is important to think in terms of market because revenue from hall hire can boost a church's bottom line at the end of the year. We don't do it for the dosh. But the dosh comes from people and people are the living stones with which, through grace, the kingdom is being constructed.

Notes

1 https://www.stbarnabasdulwich.org/st-barnabas/venue-hire-2/venue-hire (accessed 12.3.25).

2 https://stmichaels-parishchurch.org.uk/hall-hire-charges-and-tcs (accessed 12.3.25).

3 https://www.john-truscott.co.uk/content/search?SearchText=hall (accessed 12.3.25).

4 https://uk.ccli.com (accessed 12.3.25).

5 https://www.prsformusic.com (accessed 12.3.25).

6 https://www.gov.uk/government/organisations/valuation-office-agency (accessed 12.3.25).

Conclusion: Securing lasting change

We began with a tension inherent in the Christian Church from its inception. Christianity is a faith that claims to be 'in the world but not of the world' (John 17). This exhibits itself in a tradition that uses buildings for ministry. It also values metaphors of the built environment for its community, while simultaneously acknowledging that the fullness of God's kingdom will not come on earth. Christian theologians tend to position themselves towards one or other end of this spectrum. Some affirm the radical otherness of God and anticipate a future coming of the kingdom in its fullness. Others take a more incarnational approach and discern divine glory in the gritty ordinariness of everyday life.

One writer who carefully positions himself between these opposing poles is Timothy Gorringe. In *A theology of the built environment*, Gorringe draws on the thought of Karl Barth to affirm a Trinitarian faith that teaches us, through the doctrine of the Holy Spirit, to find God in all life and creativity. Gorringe also simultaneously endorses the concept of creation *ex nihilo*, such that God must be radically different from the world (Gorringe, pp. 16–17). Gorringe quotes Nicholas Lash, who writes that the doctrine of the Trinity therefore functions both

> to indicate where God is to be found and – by denying, at each point, that what we find there is to be simply identified with God – to prevent us from getting stuck in one sidedness … The doctrine thus leads at every turn, to both affirmation and denial. (Lash, p. 267)

Gorringe concludes that the result of this paradox is that

> building Jerusalem, the city of justice, peace and beauty, is a project which will never be completed this side of the kingdom, but it is a project to which we are called by the kingdom, by 'grace abounding in the lives of sinners'. (Gorringe, p. 19)

Church buildings must never be idolized as ends in themselves. As Christians, we are not interested in preserving them for their heritage alone. But we preserve their heritage because it points to something of greater and higher value: the purposes and presence of the almighty. While we acknowledge that God is invisible and omnipresent, and that our churches are the limited works of flawed creatures, we cherish them as places where, for many, God is exceptionally to be encountered.

Churches that successfully tread the tightrope between the conservation of past glories and adaptation to contemporary need will speak of the God that those churches were built to serve. We have witnessed this in three particular areas. The first is the significance of grounded community: places where people are welcomed and included, and where the gospel may be shared in word and deed. The second is as an embodied statement of the ethical values of that faith community. This truth is most obvious in the green agenda. A reduction in churches' carbon consumption is essential if Christians are to speak with integrity about contemporary issues of environmental justice and lead the world into a fairer and stabler future. Connected with this, and third, we need to attest to God's enormity by doing the right things for the long term.

Securing lasting change consonant with our claim to be in the eternity business is not easy. When individual ministers depart from a sphere of ministry, they need to lay down and hand on. During the time that we occupy a position of leadership, we have freedom to make choices and a responsibility to avoid mistakes. Our successors have the same privileges, including in relation to what they inherit from us. We must hope that steps which we have taken for the long term will be appreciated and built upon, and inspire others to follow suit. Even though we cannot tie the hands of our successors, we continue to be called to do the right thing for the long term in the context in which we find ourselves now: as part of a bigger whole, trusting to the greater purposes of God for that time after which our role in a place has come to an end.

CONCLUSION: SECURING LASTING CHANGE

The honest truth is that the implementation of many building projects may extend beyond the time, energy and money that we as individuals can put into them. And the impact of such projects is likely to stretch further still, even beyond our lifetimes. All we can do is plan and act with diligence and an awareness that we are part of a larger whole and longer story.

Salisbury Cathedral, where I am privileged to work, is the inspired design of one man, Elias of Dereham. In the early thirteenth century, he drew on new trends in gothic architecture, which he saw elsewhere in England and on the continent, to design a church that is architecturally at unity with itself. Yet Elias himself did not live to see its completion. He died in 1245. Elias's full vision was not realized until the cathedral was completed in 1258. Nonetheless, Elias' masterplan was cogent and enduring: after his death the bishop and dean did not change direction and introduce new designs.

Given this, I am acutely aware at the cathedral of playing a small role in a number of projects, each in different stages of progress. I joined the team just before the end of a major repair programme (MRP): the work of a generation to restore the external masonry and glazing of the cathedral. I felt an utter fraud when asked to bless the cross on the east end as part of the topping out ceremony, which marked the conclusion of the MRP. I knew that it was the work of countless craftspeople that had brought the organization to this point of celebration. However, I see other projects, all moving at different speeds, some of which will start and finish during my time at the cathedral; others may well be implemented by those who come after I have gone but will be dependent on the preparatory groundwork that is currently in train.

Taking the long view must therefore not become an excuse for conservative inertia. Rather, it should inspire us with a bigger picture that encourages us to persevere (James 1.3–4). The Christian quest for the stuff of eternity reaffirms our calling to do the right thing here and now. We saw this most particularly in relation to the need for everyone to reduce the consumption of carbon. The future direction of life on earth lies within the hands of each of us; Greta Thunberg is right that no one is too small to make a difference.

Alongside these long-term trends, we live in an age of rapid changes that present their own challenges. We do not want to be swept away through foolish investment in the bleeding edge of technology. However, churches that are responsive and responsible adopters of progress will not only stay ahead of the game but will also witness effectively to the contemporary relevance of the gospel they preach. Legislation is continually changing the demands laid on our buildings and how we use them. We see this, for example, in the adaptations that are being required in response to Martyn's Law, to help to increase safety against terrorism. Further changes are doubtless just around the corner.

Each church must seek the solutions that are right it; no book can suggest answers to every problem in each setting. That is why I have deliberately chosen to offer a selection of narrated examples to bring alive real-world projects that have been implemented and which are making a difference on the ground. I hope that the energy and ideas from these communities might serve as a blessing to others, including your own.

Bibliography

Websites
(accessed 12 March 2025)

General, background issues

https://www.anglicancommunion.org/mission/marks-of-mission.aspx.
https://ccx.org.uk.
https://churchofengland.org/media/press-releases/weekly-church-attendance-fivecent-third-year-consecutive-growth.
https://churchofengland.org/resources/churchcare.
https://churchofengland.org/sites/default/files/2023-06/gs-2315-mission-pastoral-measure-review_july2023-updated.pdf.
https://www.churchtimes.co.uk/articles/2024/15-march/features/features/no-churchwardens-and-vacant-pcc-posts-an-investigation-into-the-church-volunteering-crisis.
https://www.churchtimes.co.uk/articles/2024/12-april/comment/opinion/state-support-is-needed-to-keep-churches-open.
https://www.leadingyourchurchintogrowth.org.uk.
https://reports.ofsted.gov.uk/provider/21/117451.

Permissions

https://chelmsford.anglican.org/uploads-new/pages/3a_parish_user_manual_2022.pdf.
https://facultyonline.churchofengland.org/home.
https://historicengland.org.uk/listing/the-list/.

Funding

https://www.acat.uk.com/.
https://www.churchtimes.co.uk/articles/2014/7-february/news/uk/wiltshire-church-to-reap-benefits-of-sold-painting.
https://www.churchtimes.co.uk/articles/2021/4-june/comment/opinion/outward-sign-of-the-hope-of-glory.

https://www.grantfinder.co.uk/.
https://www.heritagefund.org.uk.
https://htboa.org/our-story/restoration/.
https://justgiving.com/campaign/chairsforstjohnsradlett.
https://listed-places-of-worship-grant.dcms.gov.uk/.
https://sirgarblog.blogspot.com/2011/11/official-reopening-for-st-marys-church.html.
https://www.stalbansdiocese.org/news/radlett-church-re-opens-after-major-building-project/.

Open Churches

https://enjoystalbans.com/wp-content/uploads/2019/07/PilgrimChurchesLeaflet.pdf.

Projects – toilets, kitchens, cafes, shops, offices

https://www.astorbannerman.co.uk/news/historic-bath-abbey-gets-new-changing-places-toilet/.
https://www.bathabbey.org/footprint/.
https://cathedralandchurchshops.com/index.php.
https://chalkevalleystores.co.uk/.
https://champing.co.uk/.
https://www.changing-places.org/.
https://www.churchtimes.co.uk/articles/2023/21-april/features/features/can-commerce-and-worship-co-exist-a-way-out-of-the-red-for-churches.
https://en.wikipedia.org/wiki/St_Jude%27s_Church,_Kensington.
https://www.hse.gov.uk/pubns/ck1.htm.
https://matthewshouse.org.uk/.
https://plunkett.co.uk/.
https://www.thecityofldn.com/directory/host-cafe/.
https://the-hill.co/.
https://thesherriffcentre.co.uk/.
https://www.zehnder.co.uk/en/sectors-knowledge/zehnder-academy/case-studies/st-judes-church.

Carbon reduction

https://arocha.org.uk/.
https://bristol-cathedral.co.uk/about-us/sustainability/.
https://churchofengland.org/sites/default/files/2022-06/nzc_2030_routemap_june22.pdf.
https://www.nationalgrid.com/deliveringfor2035.
https://www.svenskakyrkan.se/filer/A%20Bishop%c2%b4s%20Letter%20About%20the%20Climate.pdf.

https://www.vatican.va/content/francesco/en/encyclicals/documents/papa-francesco_20150524_enciclica-laudato-si.html.

https://historicengland.org.uk/education/training-skills/training/webinars/technical-tuesdays/.

Churchyards and land

https://www.caringforgodsacre.org.uk/.
https://www.churchofengland.org/resources/churchcare/advice-and-guidance-church-buildings/outdoor-worship.
https://engageworship.org/ideas/outdoor-worship-stations.
https://historicengland.org.uk/images-books/publications/adapting-historic-buildings-energy-carbon-efficiency-advice-note-18/.
https://www.marshalswick.org.uk/peppercornplace.htm.
https://www.northwessexdowns.org.uk/wp-content/uploads/2021/11/Lighting_Guide_07-05_MEDRES.pdf/parishbuying.org.uk/.
https://www.plantlife.org.uk/.
https://www.stalbansdiocese.org/wp-content/uploads/2024/08/JustPark-Church-Car-Parks.pdf.

Halls

https://find-mushroom.com/.
https://www.john-truscott.co.uk/.
https://www.prsformusic.com/.
https://stbarnabasdulwich.org/st-barnabas/venue-hire-2/venue-hire/.
https://www.stmichaels-parishchurch.org.uk/hall-hire-charges-and-tcs/.
https://uk.ccli.com/.

Publications

Adapting historic buildings for energy and carbon efficiency, 2024, London: Historic England, available at https://historicengland.org.uk/images-books/publications/adapting-historic-buildings-energy-carbon-efficiency-advice-note-18

Archbishops' Council, 2006, *Common Worship: times and seasons*, London: Church House Publishing.

Aston, Peter, 1976, *The true glory*, Salisbury: RSCM Press.

Bauckham, Richard, 2010, *Bible and ecology: rediscovering the community of creation*, London: Darton, Longman and Todd.

Behrens, James, 1998, *Practical church management: a guide for every parish*, Leominster: Gracewing.

Betjeman, John, 1997, *Collected poems*, 4th edn, London: John Murray.

Bishops of the Church of Sweden, 2020, *A bishops' letter about the climate*, 2nd edn, Stockholm: Åtta45, available at https://www.svenskakyrkan.se/filer/A%20Bishop´s%20Letter%20About%20the%20Climate.pdf

Bond, Paul, 2006, *Open for you: the church, the visitor and the gospel*, Norwich: Canterbury Press.

Bruce, Steve, 2002, *God is dead: secularization in the West*, Oxford: Wiley-Blackwell.

Chew, Mike, and Mark Ireland, 2009, *How to do Mission Action Planning: a vision-centred approach*, London: SPCK.

Church of England Environment Programme, 2022, *The Church of England routemap to net zero carbon by 2030*, London: Church House Publishing, available at https://www.churchofengland.org/sites/default/files/ 2022-06/nzc_2030_routemap_june22.pdf

Cocksworth, Christopher, and Rosalind Brown, 2002, *Being a priest today*, Norwich: Canterbury Press.

Coley, Lee, 12 April 2024, 'State support is needed to keep churches open', *Church Times*, available at https://www.churchtimes.co.uk/articles/2024/12-april/comment/opinion/state-support-is-needed-to-keep-churches-open

Colvin, Howard, 1983, *Unbuilt Oxford*, New Haven, CT: Yale University Press.

Cooper, Trevor, and Sarah Brown, eds, 2011, *Pews, benches and chairs: church seating in English parish churches from the fourteenth century to the present*, London: Ecclesiological Society.

Cray, Graham, *Mission-shaped Church: church planting and fresh expressions of Church in a changing context*, London: Church House Publishing.

Dark skies of the North Wessex Downs: a guide to good external lighting, 2021, Hungerford: North Wessex Downs Area of Outstanding Natural Beauty, available at northwessexdowns.org.uk/wp-content/uploads/2021/11/Lighting_Guide_07-05_MEDRES.pdf

Davie, Grace, 2002, *Europe: the exceptional case – parameters of faith in the modern world*, London: Darton, Longman and Todd.

Davies, Madeleine, 15 March 2024, 'No churchwardens and vacant PCC posts: an investigation into the church volunteering crisis', *Church Times*, available at https://www.churchtimes.co.uk/articles/2024/15-march/features/features/no-churchwardens-and-vacant-pcc-posts-an-investigation-into-the-church-volunteering-crisis

Davies, Nick, 4 June 2021, 'Outward sign of the hope of glory', *Church Times*, available at https://www.churchtimes.co.uk/articles/2021/4-june/comment/opinion/outward-sign-of-the-hope-of-glory

Donne, John, 2013, *The complete poems of John Donne*, ed. Robin Robbins, Abingdon: Routledge.

Donovan, Vincent J., *Christianity rediscovered: an epistle from the Masai*, London: SCM Press.

Francis, 2015, *Laudato Si'*, Rome: Vatican Press, available at https://www.vatican.va/content/francesco/en/encyclicals/documents/papa-francesco_20150524_enciclica-laudato-si.html

From anecdote to evidence: findings from the Church Growth Research Programme, 2011–2013, available at https://www.churchofengland.org/about/vision-strategy/funding-strategic-mission-and-ministry/strategic-development-funding/anecdote.

Giles, Richard, 2004, *Re-pitching the tent: the definitive guide to re-ordering church buildings for worship and mission*, 3rd edn, Norwich: Canterbury Press.

Gorringe, Timothy J., 2002, *A theology of the built environment*, Cambridge: Cambridge University Press.

Harvey, Michael, 2015, *Creating a culture of invitation in your church*, Oxford: Monarch.

Herbert, Shiranikha, 7 February 2014, 'Wiltshire church to reap benefits of sold painting', *Church Times*, available at https://www.churchtimes.co.uk/articles/2014/7-february/news/uk/wiltshire-church-to-reap-benefits-of-sold-painting

Holtham, Nicholas, 2022, *Sleepers wake: getting serious about climate change*, London: SPCK.

Hoyle, David, 2016, *The pattern of our calling: ministry yesterday, today and tomorrow*, London: SCM Press.

Inge, John, 2003, *A Christian theology of place*, Aldershot: Ashgate.

Jackson, Bob, 2002, *Hope for the Church: contemporary strategies for growth*, London: Church House Publishing.

Jackson, Bob, 2005 *The road to growth: towards a thriving church*, London: Church House Publishing.

Jackson, Bob, 2015, *What makes churches grow? Vision and practice in effective mission*, London: Church House Publishing.

Jackson, Bob, and George Fisher, 2009, *Everybody welcome: the course where everybody helps to grow their church*, London: Church House Publishing.

Jenkins, Simon, 2000, *England's thousand best churches*, London: Penguin.

John, Jeffrey, 2001, *The meaning in the miracles*. Norwich: Canterbury Press.

Lash, Nicholas, 1988, *Easter in ordinary: reflections on human experience and the knowledge of God*, London: SCM Press.

Mallon, James, 2014, *Divine renovation: bringing your parish from maintenance to mission*, New London, CT: Twenty-third Publications.

Miles, James, 2022, *Online faculty system: a parish user's manual – 2022 Rules*, London: Church of England and Church Buildings Division, available at https://www.chelmsford.anglican.org/uploads-new/pages/3a_parish_user_manual_2022.pdf

Mole, John, 2020, *Gold to gold*, Nottingham: Shoestring.

Murrie, Diana, 2010a, *My baptism book: a child's guide to baptism*, London: Church House Publishing.

Murrie, Diana, 2010b, *My Communion book: a child's guide to Holy Communion*, London: Church House Publishing.

Northcott, Michael S., 2009, *Environment and Christian ethics*, Cambridge: Cambridge University Press.

Percy, Emma, 2014, *What clergy do, especially when it looks like nothing*, London: SPCK.
Powell, Neil, 1998, *Selected poems*, Manchester: Carcanet.
Pritchard, John, 2007, *The life and work of a priest*, London: SPCK.
Quiller-Couch, Arthur, ed., 1939, *The Oxford book of English verse, 1250–1918*, Oxford: Clarendon Press.
Rumsey, Andrew, 2017, *Parish: an Anglican theology of place*, London: SCM Press.
Smith, Ian, 2006, *The good parish management guide: how to revive your parish*, Norwich: Canterbury Press.
Thunberg, Greta, 2019, *No one is too small to make a difference*, London: Penguin.
Tomlin, Graham, 2014, *The widening circle: priesthood as God's way of blessing the world*, London: SPCK.
Walter, Nigel, 2011, *The gate of heaven: how church buildings speak of God*, Cambridge: Grove Books.
Walter, Nigel, 2014, *Church buildings for people: reimagining church buildings as nourishing places*, Cambridge: Grove Books.
Walter, Nigel, and Andrew Mottram, 2015, *Buildings for mission: a complete guide to the care, conservation and development of churches*, Norwich: Canterbury Press.
Warren, Robert, 2004, *The healthy churches handbook*, London: Church House Publishing.
Warren, Robert, 2012, *Developing healthy churches: returning to the heart of mission and ministry*, London: Church House Publishing.
White, Robert S., ed., 2009, *Creation in crisis: Christian perspectives on sustainability*, London: SPCK.

List of images

Chapter 1

p. 2   A glimpse at the earliest Christian buildings: the house church of Dura Europos, Syria. Source: https://commons.wikimedia.org/wiki/File:DuraEuropos-Church.jpg.

p. 8   No longer in the eternity business: a derelict chapel. Source: https://www.flickr.com/photos/kelmon/11655743015

Chapter 2

p. 40   A church rebuilt through commercial partnership: St John's, Radlett (2024). Source: https://justgiving.com/campaign/chairsforstjohnsradlett.

p. 41   *Christ Blessing*: the painting that launched a transformation in Holy Trinity, Bradford-on-Avon. Source: https://www.churchtimes.co.uk/articles/2014/7-february/news/uk/wiltshire-church-to-reap-benefits-of-sold-painting.

Chapter 3

p. 51   An example of a risk assessment for unstaffed opening. Source: Kenneth Padley.

p. 57   Nothing says welcome quite like the Ecclesiastical Courts Jurisdiction Act 1860. Source: Kenneth Padley.

p. 63   Simple and inviting. Source: Kenneth Padley.

Chapter 4

p. 72   The porch of St Thomas's, Salisbury. Source: Kenneth Padley.

p. 78   The kitchen at Holy Trinity, Bradford-on-Avon. Source: Kenneth Padley.

p. 79   The kitchen at St Mary's, Marshalswick. Source: St Mary's, Marshalswick.

Chapter 5

p. 102 Air source heat pumps, discreetly located on the north roof of the chancel, Sherborne Abbey. Source: Andrew Rowland.
p. 103 Craftily disguised air-conditioning unit, Odigìtrias Monastery, Crete. Source: Kenneth Padley.
p. 107 Solar panels on Salisbury Cathedral. Source: Salisbury Cathedral.

Chapter 6

p. 123 Wildflower planting, Salisbury Cathedral. Source: Kenneth Padley.
p. 125 Building the Easter Garden: all-age worship on Good Friday, St Michael's, St Albans. Source: St Michael's with St Mary's, St Albans.
p. 127 Folk Night, St Michael's, St Albans. Source: St Michael's with St Mary's, St Albans.
p. 129 Peppercorn Place, St Mary's, Marshalswick. Source: St Mary's, Marshalswick.
p. 133 Electric-vehicle charging and bike rack proposals, Salisbury Cathedral, 2024. Source: Salisbury Cathedral.

Chapter 7

p. 141 An uninviting frontage before refurbishment: overgrown trees, a broken window, tired paintwork, an arrow-riddled door, and a tatty noticeboard at St Michael's Memorial Hall. Source: Kenneth Padley.
p. 151 St Mary's crafty infill toilet extension. Source: St Michael's with St Mary's, St Albans.

Index of Names and Subjects

access
　general 46, 63–7, 75
　hearing 65
　mobility, wheelchairs 64, 75, 113, 118, 130, 132, 150
　neuro-diversity 65
　sight 64–5, 106, 113, 119
access audit / review 66, 67
affordable housing 40, 85–6
air change cycles *see* thermal efficiency
alcohol 144
amenity societies
　local 28, 30–1
　national 29
A Rocha UK, Eco Church 110
architects 17, 25, 98, 105, 140
archaeology 25, 101, 121
arson 50–1, 58
asbestos 17, 142
Association of English Cathedrals 29

batteries 107–8
benches *see* seating
bereavement *see* death, theology of
bicycles 132
bones 121
Burial Act 1855 116, 117
burial of ashes 31, 116
business rates 146

cafés 79–81, 84–5
car parks 130–2
carbon dioxide, carbon footprint
　chapter 5, 119, 158, 159
carbon monoxide *see* fire safety
card readers 60
Care of Cathedrals Measure 29
Caring for God's Acre 122
Cathedral and Church Shops Association 83–4
Cathedrals Fabric Commission for England 29, 30
Cathedrals Measure 29
chairs *see* seating
champing 87–8
chancellors 27, 30, 31, 32
changing places *see* toilets
Charities Act 137, 148–9
children's corners 58–9
Church Care (website/YouTube) 95, 107
Church Commissioners 32, 92–3
Churches Conservation Trust 87–8
church (etymology) 1–6
churchyards
　general chapter 6
　graves, gravestones 112, 119, 128
　lighting 73, 118–19
　maintenance 17, 112–15, 118, 119, 120

pathways 17, 64, 73, 115, 118, 119, 122, 123
  walls 120
climate change 89–92
closed churches xiii, 46
closed churchyards 115–17, 119
clutter *see* storage
coefficient of performance 100
collections policy 41
condition surveys, quinquennial inspections 16, 23, 140–1
Conservation Areas 22, 119
contested heritage 110–11
coronavirus restrictions xiv, 124, 127, 153
Council for British Archaeology 29
counter-terrorism, Martyn's Law 160
creation 90–1, 123, 128

damage (accidental, deliberate) 50–1, 55–6
death, theology of 31–2, 113–14
Diocesan Advisory Committee 17, 22, 25, 27–8, 31, 32, 66, 69, 105
display screen equipment 82
district heating 103
diversifying income 137–8
diversity *see* equality, diversity, inclusion
dogs 60–1, 88
donations *see* funding
draughts *see* thermal efficiency
dual control 29
due diligence 35

Easter garden 125
ecclesiastical exemption 24, 25–6, 29, 32
ecclesiology 1–6, 48
Eco Church *see* A Rocha UK

ecology 25, 97, 119, 120, 121–3
ecumenism 87
electrical testing (fixed and portable) 16
electricity (renewable) 100, 105
electric vehicles, charging 130–2
electronic door opener 60–1
emergency lighting 17
Energy Footprint Tool / Energy Toolkit *see* carbon footprint
environment chapter 5, 112, 158
Equality Act 63–4, 75
equality, diversity, inclusion (EDI) 34, 75, 112
expectations 9–10

Fabric Advisory Committee 29
faculties *see* permissions
fallow time xiv
fire safety 16, 17
first aid 17, 77, 145
food hygiene 77, 80, 145
Forth Bridge principle 19, 154–6
friends' groups 34–5, 153
funding
  general 32–3
  donations 35–7
  fundraising 37
  grants 33–5, 141, 151–3
  legacies 37–9
  loans 41–2
  reserves 39
  sales 39–41

gardens 129, 134
gardens of remembrance *see* burial of ashes
gas safety 16
General Synod 92
Georgian Group 29
gifts (genuine and illusory) 37, 53

INDEX OF NAMES AND SUBJECTS

giving (campaigns, congregational) 13, 35–6, 38, 137
glass, glazing 71–3, 82, 99
glebe 128
grants *see* funding
graves, gravestones, graveyards *see* churchyards

halls
  administration 142–56
  building plan 141–2, 149–53
  business plan 146–53
  rates 147–8
  parking 130, 131
hearing *see* access
heating 9, 97–103, 134
heritage trusts xiv
Historic Buildings & Places (amenity society) 29
Historic England 23, 29, 30, 96
homelessness 85–6

inclusion *see* equality, diversity, inclusion
insurance, insurers 41, 49–50, 58, 61, 119, 144–5
internet 9, 60, 83, 145

Kingdom of God xiii
kitchens 76–9

leases 145–6
legacies *see* funding
lighting 44, 59, 64, 104–6, 107
listed buildings 22, 23, 74, 92, 98, 150
listed building consent *see* permissions
Liturgical Plan 29–30
loans *see* funding
long termism 6–10, 38–9, 42, 90, 97, 101, 158–60

marginal gains, Dave Brailsford 18–19
marketing *see* publicity
Martyn's Law *see* counter-terrorism
Marks of Mission 91, 109
memorials, monuments 37, 120, 121
Mission Action Plans *see* strategy
Mission and Pastoral Measure xiv
mobility *see* access
monuments *see* memorials
music performance licenses 145

National Grid 100, 105, 107
National Lottery Heritage Fund *see* funding – grants
nesting (wildlife) 121, 122
net zero *see* environment and Routemap to Net Zero
neuro-diversity *see* access
No Mow May *see* rewilding
nursery schools 146

office space 81–3, 155
open churches chapter 3, 127
open churchyards 115–17, 118
outdoor worship 123–5, 129

Parish Buying Scheme 60, 100
parish share 10, 32, 137
pathways *see* churchyards
PAT-testing *see* electrical testing
permissions
  archdeacon's letter 27
  faculty 27–32, 106
  listed building consent 29
  planning 27–32, 96, 132
perseverance 42–9
pews *see* seating
photo-voltaic cells *see* solar panels
pilgrim trails 63
planning *see* permissions
Plantlife 122

171

Plunkett Foundation 84
porches 56, 67, 71–3
portable assets *see* funding – sales
prayer cards and stands 54, 58, 60
publicity (banners, electronic, leaflets, online, posters) 56, 57, 60, 120, 137, 154

quinquennial inspections *see* condition surveys

recycling 78, 109
registrar 27, 28, 31, 120
rewilding, No Mow May 121–3
risk assessments 49–51, 145
Routemap to Net Zero 92

safeguarding 113, 143, 144
seating 64, 120, 124
sight *see* access
shops 83–5
Society for the Protection of Ancient Buildings 29
solar panels 107–8, 142
statements of need 23–4, 34
statements of significance 22–3
steps 64, 67
stewardship *see* giving
strategy, Mission Action Plans 14–15, 21–2, 36, 56, 92, 138, 148, 149
stations of the cross and resurrection 125
storage, clutter 77, 87, 120, 145
streaming (video) 145

structural engineering 25, 107

teams, team-building 24–6
Technical Tuesdays (Historic England) 96
Temporary Event Notices 144
terms and conditions of hire 143–6
theft 50–1, 55–6, 113
thermal efficiency 71, 98–9, 102
thresholds 56–7, 59, 68, 71–3, 114–15, 124, 126, 127
time and talents survey 13
toilets, changing places 65, 66, 73–6, 149–53
tourism *see* visitors
trees 112, 119, 129
Twentieth-Century Society 29

unstaffed opening *see* open churches
utility data loggers 95

Value Added Tax 74
Victorian Society 29
visitors, tourism 52–3, 56–63, 70, 77, 149
visitor book 54–5
volunteers xiv, 13, 52, 80, 114, 139–40
votive stands 58

walls *see* churchyards
welcome xvi, 47, 52, 56–61, 67, 71–3, 76–7, 99–100, 112, 141, 148–9, 158
wheelchairs *see* access
wifi *see* internet

www.ingramcontent.com/pod-product-compliance
Lightning Source LLC
Chambersburg PA
CBHW060606080526
44585CB00013B/696